ASPECTS
OF
ALCOHOLISM

Volume 2

ASPECTS

OF

ALCOHOLISM

Volume 2

With a Preface by

RUTH FOX, MD

MEDICAL DIRECTOR, THE NATIONAL COUNCIL ON ALCOHOLISM

Philadelphia   J. B. LIPPINCOTT COMPANY   *Montreal*

Distributed in Great Britain by
Pitman Medical Publishing Company, Limited, London

Library of Congress Catalog Card No. 66-14706

PRINTED IN THE UNITED STATES OF AMERICA

SP-B

PREFACE

THOUGH ALCOHOLISM is now recognized as an extremely complex disease with cultural, psychological, physiological, and spiritual overtones in a cause and effect relationship, the results of treatment have grown steadily better during the past thirty years. First, Alcoholics Anonymous showed us that alcoholism can occur in the rich or the poor, the educated or the uneducated, the gifted or the not so gifted, the important executive or the laborer—in fact, that alcoholism, being an illness, cuts across all social lines. AA taught us also that recovery is possible and that persons afflicted could resume their normal place in society, becoming again self-supporting, self-respecting, good citizens, good husbands, and good parents.

Further studies by the Yale Center of Alcohol Studies (now the Rutgers Center of Alcohol Studies at Rutgers University, New Brunswick, New Jersey), the National Council on Alcoholism and its affiliates, the various state and provincial programs, the World Health Organization and others have succeeded in breaking down the old stereotype of the alcoholic as just a worthless skid-row derelict. After recovery, many prove to be gifted, intelligent and conscientious. Having lived through the dreadful turmoil of their disease has in many cases made them more tolerant of themselves and others, more aware of their own potential as well as their limitations, and more responsive to the needs of others.

For an alcoholic to recover, he must give up all forms of alcohol for the duration of his life—not at all an easy thing to do when one considers how deeply engrained in our culture drinking is. Many people may be needed to help him to see that a life without alcohol can be happier than one with it. Here the doctor often plays one of the most crucial roles. For this reason this compilation of articles by

Roche Laboratories, which summarizes much of the up-to-date knowledge about alcoholism in its many facets, is so important. All statements are well documented, the bibliographies show an understanding of the complexity of the problem, and the writing is clear and pleasantly readable.

RUTH FOX, MD
Medical Director
The National Council on Alcoholism, Inc.
New York, New York

CONTENTS

FIGURES

TABLES

CHAPTER 1

SIGNS AND SYMPTOMS

H E MAY BE the neatly groomed professional man noted among his colleagues for his long weekends, the young salesman with yet another traffic ticket, the unkempt loiterer asking for a dime. *He* may even be a *she*—a professional woman, a housewife, a grandmother. One adult in 25 is alcoholic,[1] and the stereotyped image of alcoholic-derelict is clearly a fallacy. Most alcoholics begin as ordinary people leading ordinary lives—"respectable citizens living quietly in our communities, their alcoholism unknown to us."[2] Only as their disease progresses does their behavior change to a degree that affects their health, families, and jobs.

ON THE TRAIL OF THE ALCOHOLIC

Although socioeconomic, sex or age factors cannot be used to spot the alcoholic, certain overt signs and symptoms presented by the alcoholic point readily to his condition. And with the right technics, careful examinations, and "considerable ingenuity as well as high level of suspicion,"[2] alcoholism can usually be detected.

What first brings the alcoholic to the attention of the doctor? How can medical skills and acumen be put to use when they matter most, during the critical first stage before irreversible changes occur and dangerous medical complications develop? Rare is the alcoholic who will admit his drinking problem, rarer still he who openly seeks help. He is much more likely to come to the doctor with complaints of a different nature. He is bothered by indigestion, he has spells of nausea and diarrhea, he is concerned about weight loss, he is so plagued by anxiety and apprehension that he cannot sleep. Such presenting symptoms usually lead to a thorough examination—and here the physician can observe physical signs indicative of uncontrolled drinking.

9

WHAT CAN BE SEEN

To an alert eye, the skin of a patient may be the first indicator of alcoholism. Erratic eating habits, characteristic of the heavy drinker, are apt to produce multiple vitamin deficiencies; his lesions are primarily dermatologic, of avitaminoses and allergic manifestations. Deficiencies of thiamine chloride, riboflavin, nicotinic acid, and vitamins A and C should be considered suggestive of alcoholism. Allergic manifestations may arise from sensitization to such specific substances as the proteins of barley, malt, yeast and rye.[3] Presumably, permeability to the gastrointestinal barrier increases with alcohol ingestion, and allergens, absorbed unchanged into the circulation, lead to sensitivity reactions.

Bruises and wounds in unusual places may arouse the physician's suspicions. Such injuries are frequently self-induced, as the intoxicated person attempts "to get from the bed to the bottle." [1] And the alcoholic is known to be "somewhat more prone to infections, head injuries and other traumata than is the nonalcoholic." [3]

The patient who speaks of painful gastritis may be entirely justified in his complaints: excessive drinking can inflame the stomach and intestines so severely that digestion of food is difficult and uncomfortable. An anemic condition can evolve from a habit of prolonged, excessive drinking. While its etiology is not entirely clear, contributing factors are vitamin deficiency and gastrointestinal dysfunction, with poor iron absorption.[3] When examination of a patient reveals a palpable, enlarged liver, which cannot be explained otherwise, the physician should surely consider the possibility of alcoholism. Bates's sample of 124 male alcoholic patients showed 46% with an enlarged liver.[1] In a series conducted at another hospital—104 consecutive persons admitted for the treatment of acute alcoholism, with chronic alcoholism a concurrent diagnosis in all cases [4]—70% presented with this symptom.

Diet deficiencies, again, can be blamed when physical signs of cirrhosis appear. Pfeffer describes the liver disease usually associated with alcoholism as diffuse hepatic fibrosis-portal cirrhosis of the Laennec type. Unwilling to point to a direct etiologic relationship between alcohol and this condition, he believes the association more than "merely casual." He suggests nutritional changes as the fundamental abnormality, primarily protein and vitamin deficiencies.[3] Some of the physical signs of portal cirrhosis that Pfeffer mentions are hepatomegaly, splenomegaly, jaundice, abdominal caput, ascites, edema, spider angiomata, loss of hair, and esophageal varices. Yet, he says, symptoms of liver dysfunction are very often absent despite clear-cut objective evidence of the existence of cirrhosis.[3]

When the patient's EKG shows a tachycardia of about 110 and somatic tremor is present, the diagnosis may be thyrotoxicosis. On the other hand, if the thyroid is not palpable, such symptoms suggest an addiction, possibly alcoholic.

DEVIANT BEHAVIOR PATTERNS

Excessive, uncontrolled drinking does not leave the patient's psyche unshaken. The physician can expect to see personality and behavior patterns ranging from the mildly unusual to the wildly bizarre. Since alcohol is a drug that affects the nervous system in a manner similar to that of a general anesthetic, it depresses higher inhibitory control mechanisms, thus releases inhibitions, and affects reasoning, judgment, memory, and control.[5]

Even on first confrontation, the doctor may observe that the patient is "irritable, hostile, impulsive, and demanding," often convinced that "no one has understood him." [6] Gal further describes some of the outward behavioral manifestations of the alcoholic and possible motivations: "low frustration tolerance, feeling of isolation, and a tendency to act with rebellion. . . ." Because of his guilt feelings, he tends to "overcompensate and behave arrogantly"; underneath his arrogance, however, he desires sympathy and understanding.[6]

Psychological defects of the alcoholic are the products of defects that existed before onset of drinking, says Pfeffer, and regression is due to the drinking itself. Over a period of time, and through seemingly casual conversation, the physician may detect in his patient certain distinct personality changes. The alcoholic may show a loss of a sense of ethics, varying with periods of extreme guilt and remorse. His ability to distinguish between subjective feeling and reality may be impaired. Social involvement begins to decrease. He may lose interest in people, his work, his hobbies. Instead, he indulges in a rich fantasy life, engaging at times in various sexual and aggressive drives.[3]

THE PATIENT'S PAST

When the patient showing suggestive signs and symptoms also admits to "occasional" binges and blackouts, the physician can feel fairly certain of an alcoholic condition. Less direct information on the patient's medical and family history may warn of the problem.

If he is the child or sibling of an alcoholic or cirrhotic, the patient has a considerably higher chance of being one himself. In a study of 100 alcoholic patients, 40% had an alcoholic parent, brother or sister. The patient's record of driving accidents and arrests is also significant: in the same study, more than half the patients in the course of their drinking history had become involved with the law. Nearly 30% had been arrested more than once on the common charges of disturbing the peace or operating a motor vehicle while intoxicated.[7] In Bates's study, only one-fifth of the sample had *never* been arrested and booked for charges of being drunk and disorderly or of driving while drunk; the remainder had prison or jail records with fingerprints on file.[1]

A person's educational status apparently is not correlated with his status as a drinker. The Clancy and Vornbrock study shows their alcoholic patients equally divided between those who had terminated school at the 10th grade level, completed or nearly completed high school, and attended or graduated from college.[7] At the same time, the label of "school drop-out" should not be disregarded. In the Bates sample, 56% had left high school before getting their diplomas.[1] This, then, may be but one more factor that, when combined with others, makes for a pattern of alcoholism.

What of the patient's past illnesses and surgery? When he has had a gastric resection for intractable ulcer or pancreatitis—and especially if he is an ulcer patient who admits to drinking regularly—he is certainly a suspect for alcoholism. Tuberculosis in his medical history is a noteworthy clue: alcoholics have five times as much tuberculosis as the general population, and half the patients in a sanatorium may be alcoholic. There is also a known association between alcoholism and pneumonia.[1]

MARRIAGE AND JOB RECORDS

Although nonalcoholics are not exempt from marital discord, a divorce record should at least raise the question of alcoholism. Between 50% and 75% of all divorces arise in part from alcoholism. In the Bates study, 55% of the sample group were not living with their wives when first seen, but were bachelors or divorced men living alone or with other men; 25% were in their first divorce; about a third had been married twice or more.[1]

High rates of absenteeism and reduced efficiency in work are consequences of excessive drinking among employed alcoholics.[7] The alcoholic is frequently too intoxicated or too ill with a withdrawal hangover to work at a consistent pace. What physician is not familiar with the patient who comes in complaining of a cold, "flu," arthritis, back pain, or some other vaguely defined illness that began "a few days before"? When he asks for a written excuse from the doctor, his request may stem from the purest of motives, but he *may* be seeking a medical alibi for an alcoholic binge.

THE OVERINDULGENCE SYNDROME

Drinking and eating habits are usually interrelated. Alcoholics tend to be immoderate in these as well as in other aspects of their lives. Bates [1] refers to the "overindulgence syndrome"—excessive habits of smoking, drinking coffee, diet, and of work and sleep. Nine out of ten of his sample group smoked cigarettes: 60% of them more than a pack a day, 33% two or more packs a day. In women, even more than in men, heavy smoking can be a clue to alcoholism. The tendency to overindulge can be noted even in prescription refills; alcoholic patients have been known to double or triple their dosage of prescribed medications.[1]

Sometimes a patient's diet exposes his alcoholic problem. When he maintains his weight and the food he eats totals only a few hundred calories daily, some of his pounds may be coming from the consumption of alcohol.

ALCOHOLISM

So many signs and symptoms, apparently unrelated, may soon coalesce into an identifiable whole. A seemingly innocent annoyance, perhaps a dermatologic lesion, first brings a person into the physician's office. As the examination gets underway, the doctor may observe certain behavioral signs: excessive anxiety and tension, defensiveness, hostility clearly unprovoked. Inquiry and further examination produce more telling evidence. A recognizable pattern begins to emerge.

Diagnosis: alcoholism.

Detected in its early stages, alcoholism can be checked and some of its ravages curtailed or overcome. Alert to the myriad signals that point to the disease, the physician can do much to thwart its insidious course.

REFERENCES CHAPTER 1

1. Bates, R. C.: Appl Ther 7:466, 1965.
2. Selzer, M. L.: Industr Med Surg 30:457, 1961.
3. Pfeffer, A. Z.: Alcoholism, New York, Grune, 1958.
4. Abbott, R. R., Conboy, J. L., and Rekate, A. C.: J Mich Med Soc 62:990, 1963.
5. Karolus, H. E.: Illinois Med J 120:96, 1961.
6. Gal, P. J.: J Amer Geriat Soc 12:1128, 1964.
7. Clancy, J., and Vornbrock, R.: J Iowa Med Soc 55:235, 1965.

CHAPTER 2

WHO WILL BE AN ALCOHOLIC?

THAT ALCOHOLISM and its problems weigh on the American conscience was acknowledged at the 1964 Republican National Convention. The delegates adopted a resolution calling for Federal support of a research program aimed at the prevention and treatment of alcoholism, among other disorders.[1]

If such a program is initiated, researchers will find that much has been written about the subject [2-18] and that opinion is often speculative and contradictory. Nevertheless, there are certain broad areas of agreement. It is widely accepted, for example, that alcoholism is a disease entity [2, 14] or possibly the symptom of a disease.[15] Further, alcoholism, like other illnesses, has certain distinctive features.[2, 3, 5-7, 14, 15, 17] It has an etiology, a prognosis, a recommended treatment, and it can be defined.[3, 15, 17] An alcoholic is ". . . a person who has lost control of the practice of drinking alcoholic beverages to an extent that his interpersonal, family, or community relationships have become seriously threatened or disturbed." [3]

The disease becomes established as a result of three or four factors which operate concurrently and complement one another.[3, 5-7, 8, 18] Once started, alcoholism in the form of "symptomatic" drinking (symptomatic of some underlying psychological or social anomaly) runs a course that consists of several progressively worsening phases.[5-7, 16] In sequence, these are the *prodromal* phase, the *crucial* or *basic* phase, and the *chronic phase*. The last is characterized by deterioration of the personality and by nameless fears and tremors, reaching a climax with a series of drinking bouts, each undertaken to dispel painful memories of bad behavior during the previous bout (see Fig. 1). The remorseful aspect of alcoholism appears in Diana Barrymore's confession: "The

15

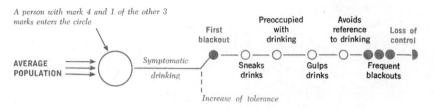

MARKED POPULATION
1. Neurosis or neurotic response pattern
2. Personality inadequacy
3. Psychotic/psychopathologic personalities
4. Hypothetical constitutional liability

PRODROMAL PHASE

Drinking is not conspicuous, and intoxications—limited to evenings except perhaps for weekends—are not severe.

A person with mark 4 and 1 of the other 3 marks enters the circle

AVERAGE POPULATION

Symptomatic drinking

First blackout

Preoccupied with drinking

Avoids reference to drinking

Loss of control

Sneaks drinks

Gulps drinks

Frequent blackouts

Increase of tolerance

CRUCIAL OR BASIC PHASE

Intoxications are the rule, but are still limited to evenings, with hangover the following mornings; onset of solitary drinking varies greatly from one drinker to another, usually occurs in basic phase.

ALCOHOL ADDICTION

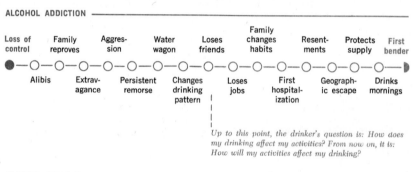

Loss of control | Family reproves | Aggression | Water wagon | Loses friends | Family changes habits | Resentments | Protects supply | First bender

Alibis | Extravagance | Persistent remorse | Changes drinking pattern | Loses jobs | First hospitalization | Geographic escape | Drinks mornings

Up to this point, the drinker's question is: How does my drinking affect my activities? From now on, it is: How will my activities affect my drinking?

ALCOHOL ADDICTION

CHRONIC PHASE

With tolerance decreased, drinking becomes nearly constant and the drinker moves on to defeat.

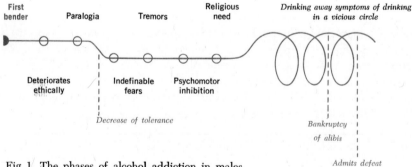

First bender | Paralogia | Tremors | Religious need | *Drinking away symptoms of drinking in a vicious circle*

Deteriorates ethically | Indefinable fears | Psychomotor inhibition

Decrease of tolerance

Bankruptcy of alibis

Admits defeat

Fig 1. The phases of alcohol addiction in males

moment I got sober I became so horrified at my behavior that I got drunk again. . . ." [11]

That alcoholics are not necessarily derelicts, moral perverts or denizens of "skid row" is also generally recognized. On the contrary, alcoholics are often family people—decent, well-meaning, employed and employable men and women.[4] Often they function on a higher level of intelligence and sensitivity than other members of the community.[17] It should be noted that most of the literature is devoted to studies of the male rather than the female alcoholic,[15] possibly because male alcoholics are more conspicuous, present a graver problem to the community, and may outnumber the female alcoholics by about 5 or 6 to one. As Gelber [15] says, ". . . little is known about women alcoholics and . . . fruitful investigation is yet to be made in many vital areas."

WHAT FACTORS LEAD TO ALCOHOLISM?

Investigators [3-5, 7, 8, 18] point out that alcoholism is a chronic illness that probably springs from the interplay of at least three conditions operating concurrently. Jellinek,[5-7] in particular, is an exponent of this thesis. He contends that no one factor acting alone can account for the onset of the drinking habit in any given individual, but that three circumstances, interweaving and reenforcing one another, must be held accountable. He has formalized and schematized this theory and presented it in the form of a table. Although somewhat mechanical, the presentation has the virtue of clarity and removes the alcohol syndrome from the realm of the mysterious.

The predisposing factors that could lead to alcoholism are *1.* a "*constitutional liability* factor," 2. a *personality* or *psychological* factor, and 3. a *social* factor. Assuming that an individual is flawed by the first two, exposing him to the social factor provides the convivial setting that encourages "symptomatic drinking." It lasts from a few months to two years, is marked by a progressive tolerance to alcohol, and leads insensibly to the prodromal phase of addiction.

1. The constitutional liability factor. This factor is hypothetical. It postulates that certain individuals have an inborn vulnerability to the action of alcohol.[5-7] More readily than other drinkers, these people lose control of their alcoholic intake because of a biochemical sensitivity to the substance. Such sensitivity may be hereditary or congenital [7] and, theoretically, may have its roots in nutritional deficiency, brain pathol-

ogy, or endocrine dysfunction. Is the constitutional liability factor due
to a so-called "inborn error of metabolism"? Considerable research now
going on is aimed at providing clues to an eventual answer.

2. *The personality or psychological factor.* Concerning the existence
of this factor and its dynamism, all students of the subject, including
Jellinek,[5-7] agree. Psychological strain, a sense of personal inadequacy,
and an estrangement from and rejection by the rest of society are
among the personality traits of the "psychologically vulnerable" individuals—men and women accustomed to taking alcohol as a solution to
personal problems. If they are also physiologically vulnerable (the
constitutional liability factor), they are in double jeopardy.

One investigator puts it this way:

The most important common factor seems to be that of a certain lack of
balance and harmony in the emotional and volitional sides of the mind—in
our psychiatric terminology: many of them are psychopaths or deviating
personalities. . . . These people suffer from feelings of inferiority and insuffi-
ciency, with frequent depressive spells. They are poor mixers, unable to assert
themselves among friends, and therefore tend to withdraw into a loneliness
which they feel very keenly.[6]

The investigator explains that alcohol has an almost specific effect
on the personality difficulties of such subjects. It gives them the confi-
dence that they seek, helping them to overcome their inhibitions. In
particular, alcohol makes it possible for such persons to associate with
other people without shyness and inferiority feelings. He also describes
an "extreme opposite" type of vulnerable personality. He is the

easy-going, friendly and sociable fellow, habitually somewhat above the
average in mood and activity, and correspondingly somewhat lacking in insight and inhibitions. He starts as a social drinker—and a careless one, because
of his blindness for his own weakness of character. Usually there is a definite
deficit of perseverance and planning—he lives for the moment, but has a low
tolerance for unpleasant experience.[6]

"*Alcoholic*" *or* "*prealcoholic personalities.*" Some investigators [13] ap-
ply such terms to these individuals, but their concept has not gone
unchallenged. Others [4, 15] maintain that prealcoholics and alcoholics
present such a broad spectrum of personality traits that no single phrase
can adequately describe or delineate those persons who turn to alcohol
as a refuge from psychic distress.

Women alcoholics don't differ markedly from men, it appears, in personality traits.[9-11] Lonelier, perhaps, and even more sensitive than the
males (". . . a vacuum in their lonely lives that they desperately try to

fill with a bottle"[9]), they tend to start drinking later in life and then go downhill faster. The woman alcoholic, too, "is usually a perfectionist who swings wildly from one emotional extreme to the other."[9]

3. The social factor. A folkway in many social circles, the consumption of alcoholic beverages with friends, associates and relatives brings a "small social reward": acceptance by the group and approbation.[4] If, then, a subject is "marked" by *1.* an endogenous sensitivity to alcohol and *2.* a personality inadequacy, and if *3.* he enters a circle of social drinkers, the stage is set for the onset of symptomatic drinking. Drinking at bars, dinner parties, luncheons, cocktail parties [5-7] and fraternities,[12] this individual gains considerable relief from his personality problems and psychological tensions. Gaining satisfaction from his initial experiences with alcohol and heartened by the conviviality, he makes the rounds. The picture of the flawed individual turned symptomatic drinker by the social milieu is poignantly painted by McGenty.[4]

The alcoholic does not know this has happened to him, is happening to him. He knows only the pain—the constant psychic pain and desperate loneliness.

One day by chance he discovers culturally available alcohol. It is a magic elixir—to him, not of intoxication but of elation. Instantly tension is relaxed. Gone suddenly is nagging insecurity. Elation brings an immediate sense of grandiosity, of omnipotence. No more dependence. The mouse becomes a giant, a demi-god striding the universe.

What mortal—without extraordinary insight, without especial grace—would not trade a life of unbearable psychic pain for a magic elixir of elation, an instantaneous sedative avenue of escape into pleasure—even if that pleasure is only the temporary cessation of pain?

What lies ahead, according to Jellinek,[5-7] is the prospect of 10 to 25 years of alcoholism during which the subject goes through three successive stages. If the habit is not broken somewhere along the line, the individual ultimately reaches the last stage, marked by ethical bankruptcy, admission of defeat, and a sincere desire for treatment.

REFERENCES CHAPTER 2

1. NY Times: News release, July 13, 1964, p. 1.
2. Queries and Minor Notes: What do you mean? Alcoholism is a disease, JAMA *164*:505, 1957. Reprinted by the Nat'l Council on Alcoholism, NY.
3. Zappala, A., and Ketcham, F. S.: Toward sensible rehabilitation of the alcoholic, Pub Health Rep *69*:1187, 1954.
4. McGenty, D.: Family relationships contributing to alcoholism. Paper read at 19th An'l Convention of Amer Catholic Sociological Soc, Trinity College, Washington (DC), Dec 28-30, 1957.

5. Jellinek, E. M.: Quart J Stud Alcohol *13*:673, 1952.

6. European Seminar and Lecture Course on Alcoholism: Sponsored by World Health Organization, Copenhagen, Denmark, Oct 22–Nov 3, 1951.

7. Jellinek, E. M.: Chart summarizing lectures (see ref 6).

8. Demone, H. W.: New Hampshire Bull on Alcoholism *12*:1 (Apr), 1963.

9. Murray, D.: The Housewife's Secret Sickness, Saturday Evening Post, Jan 27, 1962, p. 80.

10. Roth, L.: I'll Cry Tomorrow, New York, Fell, 1954.

11. Barrymore, D., and Frank, G.: Too Much, Too Soon, New York, Holt, 1961.

12. Gusfield, J. R.: Science Service, Washington (DC), Aug 31, 1961.

13. World Wide Med News Serv, Inc, NY: Report 1031, Apr 13, 1956.

14. What You Should Know About Alcoholism: US Dept of Health, Education and Welfare, Public Health Serv Pub 93, rev 1954, Washington (DC), 1954.

15. Gelber, I.: Alcoholism in NY City, Dept of Health, City of NY, 1960.

16. NY Times: News release, June 21, 1964, p. 46.

17. Mann, M.: How To Know An Alcoholic, New York, Rinehart, 1958.

18. Rothstein, C., and Siegel, P.: J Maine Med Ass *55*:128, 1964.

CHAPTER 3

PROFILE OF AN ALCOHOLIC

N UMEROUS INVESTIGATORS have attempted to establish a clear picture of the alcoholic and, perhaps even more important, of the prealcoholic personality. Results have been suggestive but inconclusive. One of the conclusions of the five-year alcoholism research program at Cornell was that "alcoholism is not a single entity or disease, but a symptom associated with several illnesses or syndromes." Indeed, in a series of 161 patients studied, the "symptom" was associated with 11 different diagnostic categories, including manic-depressive reactions, poorly organized psychoneurotic psychopathic personality, the rigidly organized obsessive-compulsive personality, and paranoid schizophrenia.[1]

PSYCHOLOGICALLY VULNERABLE

Yet if the alcoholic cannot be described precisely, the great majority seem to have in common four or five personality traits, and from these a recognizable, albeit sketchy, profile of the alcoholic can be drawn.

Low capacity for handling tensions. The trait most often noted by those who work with chronic alcoholics is the alcoholic's inability to cope with tensions. Anything that creates tension—anger, anxiety, hostility, frustration—appears to be the Achilles' heel of the alcoholic. For example, while studying 61 alcoholic outpatients, a team of investigators recorded such capsule clinical judgments as: *"Has a low threshold for feeling rejected." "Has a readiness to withdraw or become disorganized in the face of frustration and adversity." "Tends to side-step troublesome situations, makes concessions to avoid unpleasantness." "Tends to delay or avoid decision; fears committing self in any definite course of action; vacillates."* [2]

Fox and Lyon [3] point out that the extremely low tension-tolerance of many alcoholics is also characteristic of the infant; when the infant experiences tension, because of hunger, perhaps, he demands immediate relief. Similarly, the alcoholic reacts as swiftly, and almost as passionately, when things go wrong in *his* life.

Dependency. The traits most characteristic of the alcoholic, it has been suggested, are all vestigial traces of infancy. Dependency, as a trait, is certainly regressive, and the chronic alcoholic notoriously seeks to be taken care of, either by other people or by institutions. Zwerling,[4] who intensively studied a group of 46 alcoholic men, noted that his subjects tended to "lean" on people. One frankly admitted, "You might say it's a parasitic existence. I depend on my mother for everything." Many of these patients found relief for their dependency needs in Alcoholics Anonymous, one describing his feeling for the organization in this way: "We have to believe in someone stronger than ourselves to look after us and take care of us."

Hostility. Alcoholics often show evidence of marked hostility toward those closest to them. Perhaps because they are so dependent, however, this hostile core is usually repressed. One alcoholic patient, for instance, who consciously believed that he loved his overstrict mother, informed the investigator that, "She died of a stroke—just like Stalin." [4] Some of the excessive guilt and remorse suffered by many alcoholics stems from the partial release of this hostility under the influence of liquor; they remember "murderous" dreams and hallucinations experienced during a drinking bout or are mortally afraid of what they may have done during an alcoholic blackout. Occasionally, repressed hostility actually does break out during an acute intoxication stage—one of Zwerling's patients was stopped just as he was trying to push his father out of a hotel room window. By and large, though, the behavior of an alcoholic does not appear to change radically when he is drunk. (See Table 1.)

Egocentricity. Egocentricity is the fourth trait frequently ascribed to the alcoholic. Characteristically, he is wrapped up in his own problems and concerns, and largely indifferent to the needs of others. Even those who are outwardly sociable often remain essentially estranged from other people, emotionally separate from them. Fox and Lyon [3] note that this egocentricity is closely akin to the primary narcissism seen in early infancy when, for the baby, recognition of his own needs and their gratification is the only reality.

In addition to possessing these particular traits, the alcoholic also shows signs of *neurotic intrapsychic conflicts.* At least when seen by the physician, he usually appears depressed, tense, fearful and pessi-

TABLE 1. *The alcoholic when drinking: Behavioral tendencies in order of importance* °

BEHAVIORAL ITEMS	ALCOHOLIC RANKS HIMSELF	INFORMANT RANKS ALCOHOLIC
1. I feel guilty about what I'm doing	1	1
2. I say angry or insulting things to some people	4	2
3. I spend a lot of money or give things away	3	3
4. I just want to be by myself	2	7
5. I cry or feel very sad	5	4
6. I look for somebody to talk to and tell my troubles to	8	6
7. I like people to take care of me	10	5
8. I like to be the center of attraction	9	9
9. I want to have sexual intercourse	6.5	13
10. I find myself attracted to the opposite sex	6.5	15
11. I become silly or clown around	11.5	10
12. I offer to fight somebody	14	8
13. I hurt myself by accident or intentionally	11.5	11
14. I get into scraps or fights	15	12
15. I destroy, break, or harm objects	13	14
16. I take off my clothes or exhibit myself	17	16
17. I find myself attracted to persons of the same sex	16	17

° In the study by Korman and Stubblefield [2] of 61 outpatients, each patient and an outside informant, usually a friend or relative, were asked to indicate the degree to which he showed each of 17 behavioral tendencies when drinking. The investigators found no dramatic change in the alcoholic's behavior from what they would have expected from his personality.

mistic. These characteristics were noted in typical capsule judgments [2] made of individual patients: *"Has a readiness to become depressed." "Is generally nervous, tense in manner." "Is restless." "Is vulnerable to real or fancied threats; generally fearful; is a worrier." "Has feelings of inadequacy, inferiority and insecurity."* In some cases, strong feelings of depression and self-loathing can lead to suicide attempts or to "accident proneness." At least eight of Zwerling's [4] 46 patients had definitely tried to kill themselves at one time or another and a larger number— though denying any thought of suicide—had been involved in dangerous and potentially self-destructive behavior.

So the profile of the alcoholic emerges. Generally speaking, he is self-centered, dependent (but bitterly resentful of his dependency), fearful, and has difficulty in coping with the tensions of everyday life. A widely held psychoanalytic theory explains why he might easily turn to alcohol for solace. Deep in the subconscious of every individual is the memory of the "magically" relieved severe tension. When, as an infant, the individual was hungry, anxious and alone, the fluid suddenly appeared. It fed him, warmed him and soothed his fears, all at the same time. Now, as an adult, very few substances come even close to fulfilling these functions. Of these, alcohol is at once the most potent, easily accessible and socially approved substitute available.

PHYSIOLOGICALLY VULNERABLE

It is easy enough to see how psychologically vulnerable people might be motivated to use the tension-reducing properties of alcohol more frequently and in greater quantities than others. Nevertheless, certainly not all who possess these "predisposing" traits drink to excess—and of those who do, not all can be considered alcohol addicts. To explain why certain individuals, and not others, eventually lose all control over their drinking, a number of investigators insist that—along with psychological vulnerability—there must be a physiologic vulnerability as well. Certain lesions or anomalies, they believe, must be present in the individual, either inborn or acquired through heavy alcohol intake, to produce actual addiction. Some of their theories on alcoholism etiologies center on three disorders.

Nutritional deficiency. One school holds that enzyme deficiencies, in particular, may be involved in the craving for alcohol. Part of this theory is based on evidence from controlled studies in which animals had been given vitamin-deficient diets, followed by a choice of alcohol or water to drink. Mardones [5] and his associates were among the first to observe that certain diets—notably those deficient in vitamin B complex—increased alcohol intake in rats. They ascribed this increase in voluntary alcohol consumption to lack of a specific factor, which they termed N_1, and to thiamine deficiency. Some strains of rats were more prone than others to respond to N_1 deprivation, suggesting a genetic factor also at work.

The well-known genetotrophic theory of Williams,[6] who performed similar animal studies, placed greater stress on the importance of this genetic factor, the core of his formulation being the idea of "metabolic individuality" (largely genetically determined), which predisposes some individuals to alcoholism. Williams believes that there is a need for alcohol in certain individuals and that this need is derived from nutritional faults, which, in turn, are mainly due to anomalies in their enzyme systems.

Brain pathology. Encephalographic studies made during the last ten years indicate that some brain damage may result from heavy alcohol intake. Tumarkin and his co-workers,[8] for instance—who found evidence of cerebral cortical atrophy in [7] fairly young male alcoholics—theorized that repeated, severe intoxication may result in permanent and perhaps cumulative loss of cells and nerve fibers in the cerebral cortex. This could then lead to loss of tolerance to alcohol and to psychological changes, such as impoverished powers of judgment, which would result in eventual inability to control drinking. In 1956, Lemere [9] suggested that excessive use of alcohol not only damages cortical cells but also changes the metabolic pattern of brain cells so that the presence of alcohol becomes necessary for optimal brain functioning. Sudden withdrawal of alcohol then throws the brain cells into disequilibrium, which brings about a cellular craving for alcohol.

Endocrinologic dysfunction. Endocrine disturbances are often mentioned as possible forerunners of alcoholism. J. J. Smith [10] carried out one of the first thorough clinical surveys on the endocrine aspects of alcoholism. This led him to the belief that an underlying metabolic disturbance—involving interactions of the pituitary, adrenal and gonadal systems—preceded alcohol addiction. The outstanding feature of the alcoholic's disturbed metabolic pattern, according to Smith, is exhaustion of the adrenal, which is secondary to a pituitary deficiency. Other investigators have also noted adrenal anomalies in some chronic alcoholics.

Whether these or other physiologic factors render one individual more susceptible to alcohol addiction than another has not yet been proved. Those who believe that only psychological stresses lead to alcoholism argue that the physiologic anomalies so far uncovered are end-products of excessive alcohol intake rather than causes. Those in the physilogic camp point out that psychological stresses cannot explain loss of control, craving, and withdrawal symptoms. A good many investigators would take the middle road and hold that both psychological and physiologic vulnerability must be present to produce true alcohol addiction. As Lovell suggests: "The alcoholic is afflicted with a neurosis plus a sensitivity to alcohol. The sensitivity is the physical basis of his disease; without it his neurosis will not lead to compulsive drinking. On the other hand, the sensitivity in the absence of an neurosis probably will make an abstainer rather than an alcoholic." [11]

REFERENCES CHAPTER 3

1. Sherfey, M. J.: *in* Diethelm, O., ed.: Etiology of Chronic Alcoholism, Springfield (Ill.), Thomas, 1955.

2. Korman, M., and Stubblefield, R. L.: JAMA *178*:1184, 1961.

3. Fox, R., and Lyon, P.: Alcoholism—Its Scope, Cause and Treatment, New York, Random House, 1955.

4. Zwerling, I.: Quart J Stud Alcohol *20*:543, 1959.

5. Mardones, R. J.: Quart J Stud Alcohol *12*:563, 1951.

6. Williams, R. J.: Alcoholism, The Nutritional Approach, Austin, Univ Texas Press, 1959.

7. Lester, D., and Greenberg, L.: Quart J Stud Alcohol *13*:553, 1952.

8. Tumarkin, B., Wilson, J. D., and Snyder, G.: US Armed Forces Med J *6*:67, 1955.

9. Lemere, F.: Amer J Psychiat *113*:361, 1956.

10. Smith, J. J.: Quart J Stud Alcohol *10*:251, 1949.

11. Lovell, H. W.: Hope and Help for the Alcoholic, Garden City, Doubleday, 1951.

CHAPTER 4

THE "INTELLIGENT" ALCOHOLIC—WHY DOES HE DRINK?

I DRINK, states one kind of alcoholic patient, in effect, "because I am more creative, more intelligent—and therefore more high-strung—than other people. Alcohol gives me the stimulation I need to cope with the mediocrity that surrounds me." The belief that the creative person has greater need to insulate his "sensitive" nerves with alcohol is a popular one. And while it is true that a good many alcoholics are both dullards and thick-skinned, perhaps just as many alcoholics have been brilliant enough to achieve a considerable measure of success in life. In his *Cup of Fury*, for instance, Upton Sinclair [1] discusses a tragically long list of friends and acquaintances who, directly or indirectly, destroyed themselves through excessive drinking.

William Sidney Porter (O. Henry) had to be sobered up before he could write many of his famous short stories. Stephen Crane, after falling ill in Cuba, took to drinking heavily as a "cure" and was dead at 29. Eugene V. Debs was a fiery orator and a truly gentle soul but a captive of alcohol. "When Gene went on lecture tours, he was accompanied by a strong man whose major duty was to keep him fit to go on the platform." Sinclair Lewis ended a brilliant career by drinking a quart of brandy a day, wandering over the earth, avoiding his friends and desperately seeking peace. Maxwell Bodenheim, a handsome, striking man when young and author of several best-selling novels, spent his last few years wandering through Greenwich Village, posing as a blind man to pick up some coins or offering to write "poetry" for tourists in return for a drink. Hart Crane, a confirmed and hopeless alcoholic at 33, dove from a steamer into the Caribbean Sea. Ambrose Bierce, a heavy-drinking and tormented man, wandered off into Mexico, then aflame

with war and banditry, and died in a manner unreported and still unknown. F. Scott Fitzgerald wasted so much of his life on alcohol that
he was known to his friends as "F. Scotch Fitzgerald." Sinclair men-
tons others as well—Edna St. Vincent Millay, Eugene O'Neill, Finley
Peter Dunne, George Sterling, William Seabrook, Sherwood Anderson,
John Barrymore, Douglas Fairbanks, Sr., Isidora Duncan—all enormously talented and successful people who nevertheless spent a good
part of their days as victims of alcoholism.

SUICIDE BY INCHES

It sometimes seems as if the alcohol addict is deliberately bent on
destroying himself, on alienating his family and friends and ruining
both his career and his reputation. And, in the view of Karl Menninger,[2]
chronic alcoholism should actually be termed chronic suicide, that
form of self-destruction in which individuals commit suicide by inches.
Certainly, alcoholics are preoccupied, even in their sober moments,
with thoughts of self-destruction. Jack London,[3] for instance, who described his struggles with alcohol in the book *John Barleycorn,* observed that "suicide, quick or slow, a sudden spill or a gradual oozing
away, is the price John Barleycorn exacts. No friend of his ever escapes
making the just due payment." And though London promised at the
end of his book, "I will drink, but, oh, more skillfully, more discreetly
than ever before. Never again will I be a peripatetic conflagration," he
continued to drink as recklessly as before and, in less than 3 years, did
take his own life.

Other alcoholics prefer the less overt form of suicide. Like Dylan
Thomas, they simply continue to drink in the full knowledge that they
are endangering their lives. J. M. Brinnin,[4] who accompanied Thomas
on his lecture tours of the United States, reports that the famous Welsh
poet drank steadily despite occasional attacks of coughing followed by
severe retching and vomiting. "I think I have cirrhosis of the liver," the
poet informed Brinnin after one of these attacks, but he refused to cut
down on his drinking. Significantly, one of the last things he said before going into a fatal alcoholic coma was, "I want to go to the Garden
of Eden—to die . . . to be forever unconscious."

Both Lillian Roth and Diana Barrymore also continued to drink after
being warned that it might mean their deaths. Lillian Roth heard a
medical verdict of impending blindness, the onset of cirrhosis, advanced
colitis and a form of alcoholic insanity. Despite this, she continued to

drink for several years, at one point crying, "I've got to finish the bottle. I don't care what happens. I've got to finish the bottle. I want death." [5] Fortunately, with help, Miss Roth eventually managed to shake free from her addiction. Diana Barrymore, however, heard roughly the same verdict from her doctor. "You're on a dreadful merry-go-round—alcohol, barbiturates, stimulants. If you don't get off it quickly, you will die." [6] Despite a desperate struggle and occasional success, the actress never really managed to get off that merry-go-round. She died at the age of 38.

FLIGHT FROM DISEASE

Why did these and other highly intelligent people become addicted to alcohol? Each person might have offered a different excuse. According to Karl Menninger,[2] the alcoholic suffers secretly from an unspeakable terror that he cannot bear to face. Further, whatever excuse he may give, he often doesn't know the actual nature of the dreadful pain and fear within him that impels him to alcoholic self-destruction. Menninger suggests, then, that alcohol addiction is not a disease, but rather a suicidal flight from disease, a disastrous attempt at the self-cure of an unseen inner conflict. It stems from the underlying feeling of insecurity that grips even the outwardly successful alcoholic, and it is this feeling that must constantly be denied, compensated for, or anesthetized.

The "outward success" is particularly vulnerable when fears that his creative powers are starting to fade. F. Scott Fitzgerald apparently had begun drinking as a young man because in those days, he said, everyone drank. He enjoyed life in those days, however, and felt that all he needed to make a living was pencil and paper. "But then I found I needed liquor, too," he told a friend. "I needed it to write." [7] He began to drink more and more to escape the growing sense of his wasted potentiality, and also to escape strong feelings of guilt concerning his young wife who had become insane. William Seabrook described the feelings of a frustrated writer in his autobiography, *No Hiding Place*. "I was miserable . . . and before I knew it, I was drinking again in the mornings when I didn't want to drink, not for the pleasure but in the desperate false hope that I might write a page or two that wasn't wooden." [8]

Judging from their writings, the pattern of alcoholism for these creative people is the familiar one: strong feelings of inferiority even as a child; drinking begun because it seems "the thing to do" socially; the passage of several years before alcohol really takes hold. Diana Barrymore might have been speaking for any number of female alcoholics when she wrote: "As a child I'd been around clever, cultured people, but I never felt part of them. The few times I came downstairs to meet mother's famous literary friends, I'd felt . . . frightened and an impostor. . . . Now the same sense of inadequacy swept over me. Trying to be what people expected, I reached for the quip. . . . A few drinks helped things along. . . ." [6] Jack London, like many alcoholics, admitted that he never liked the taste of alcohol. But in his youth, he found that saloons were desirable places, brightly lit and cheerful, full of warmth and good fellowship. It was after years of social drinking that he found he had to drink. "I was carrying a beautiful alcoholic conflagration around with me. The thing fed on its own heat and flamed the fiercer. There was no time in all my waking time that I didn't want to drink." [3]

THE SLOW ROAD TO SELF-DESTRUCTION

For most alcoholics, the amount of liquor that must be consumed appears to grow steadily. At first, Lillian Roth observes,[5] beer by day and liquor by night satisfied her. But then her nerves seemed to demand more, and she switched from a morning beer to two ounces of bourbon in her morning orange juice. This satisfied her for a while—but one morning, while out shopping with a friend, she had a dizzy spell and almost collapsed. The friend hurried her to a cab and the experienced driver, taking one look at her, advised a quick drink." Take a tip," he advised her, "and carry a shot or two with you in the future." Miss Roth realized then that the physical demand was growing—that it was dangerous for her even to leave the house without carrying an emergency supply of liquor with her. That day, she bought some 2-ounce medicine bottles in the drug store, filled them with liquor, and thereafter was never without a couple in her purse. The 2-ounce bottles gradually became full-sized fifths. After years of steadily increasing consumption, additional punishment for the desperately sick woman came, inevitably, in the form of "the shakes," with its concomitant physical agony. She was in constant pain—in eyes, nose, sinuses, head, throat, chest, stomach, legs. Only liquor could relieve it, but her body rejected liquor. "After the shakes, of course, came delirium tremens. . . ." [5]

Yet, despite the physical and mental torture the alcoholic suffers, he continues to drink. And one reason for this, Menninger[2] suggests, is that his deep feelings of inferiority, sinfulness and unworthiness lead him naturally to think of suicide. When the individual is threatened with destruction by his own impulses, he may choose alcoholism as a kind of lesser self-destruction serving to avert the greater self-destruction.

These feelings of inferiority, in this psychiatrist's view, are based on fear and guilt induced by the feelings of rage, frustration, envy or hostility that the individual experienced as a child. All children meet with frustration and disappointment that cause them to have ambivalent feelings toward their parents. With an alcoholic, however, there apparently is a qualitative difference. The disappointments he suffers as a child become more than he can bear. His suffering is so great that he remains all his life an "oral character," never completely outgrowing that stage in his psychological development in which the child's attitude toward the world is determined by his wish to take it in through the mouth and to destroy with his mouth anything which resists his demands.

To punish loved ones by eating and drinking, or by *not* eating and drinking, is a typical infantile revenge reaction. Since the alcoholic suffers conflicting feelings of love and hate toward his family because of early disappointments, real and imaginary, he wants to punish them—but, at the same time he feels guilty about his desires. Alcoholism, therefore, serves many purposes: it is a passive form of aggression toward others; it punishes the individual for his own repressed hostilities; and it keeps him from the even greater self-punishment of *total* self-destruction.[2]

REFERENCES CHAPTER 4

1. Sinclair, U.: The Cup of Fury, New York, Channel Press, 1956.
2. Menninger, K. A.: Man Against Himself, New York, Harcourt, 1938.
3. London, J.: John Barleycorn, New York, Appleton, 1938.
4. Brinnin, J. M.: Dylan Thomas in America, Boston, Little, 1955.
5. Roth, L.: I'll Cry Tomorrow, New York, Fell, 1954.
6. Barrymore, D., and Frank, G.: Too Much, Too Soon, New York, Holt, 1957.
7. Graham, S., and Frank, G.: Beloved Infidel, New York, Holt, 1958.
8. Seabrook, W.: No Hiding Place, *in* Sinclair, U.: *op. cit.*

CHAPTER 5

INTERNATIONAL PROBLEM, DRINKING

B ECAUSE ALCOHOLIC BEVERAGES are freely available in most countries (and at least procurable in others), the alcoholic obviously may be encountered almost anywhere in the world. Yet he apparently is seen much more frequently in some countries than in others. Moreover, the public's attitude toward his condition, the medical treatment of it and, in some cases, the basic underlying causes for its onset also may differ from one country to the next. Even the term "alcoholism" itself may have various meanings to foreign experts on the subject, and Jellinek suggests that the meaning of the word be extended beyond the conception current in America and some Anglo-Saxon countries. Pointing out that there is not just one form of alcoholism but several, Jellinek has described the most common "species" of alcoholism as [1]:

Alpha alcoholism, a purely psychological dependence on alcohol for relief of bodily or emotional pain and with no signs of progression;
Beta alcoholism, in which the complications of alcoholism, such as gastritis, may occur simply because of heavy social drinking and with no signs of physical or psychological dependence;
Gamma alcoholism, in which both psychological and physical dependence are observed, the physical dependence being characterized by "loss of control"; and
Delta alcoholism, in which both psychological and physical dependence are observed, but in which physical dependence is characterized by an "inability to abstain" from alcohol rather than by a "loss of control."

Because Gamma alcoholism is, of course, the species that predominates in the United States, the tendency may be to consider it the only form of alcoholism. But in many countries, more serious problems may arise from one of the other types.

INVETERATE DRINKER—NEVER DRUNK, NEVER SOBER

Delta alcoholism, rather than Gamma, apparently predominates in France and in several other wine-drinking countries, such as Chile and Portugal. In these countries, a fairly steady morning-to-evening drinking pattern is common, and there is general social acceptance of large individual consumption. For instance, in a French survey carried out in 1953, answers by men to the question of what amount of wine a working man could drink every day "without any inconvenience" averaged 1.8 liters (slightly under 2 quarts).[2] And a hard-drinking French citizen, particularly one who works in the wine-growing area, often drinks as much as 3 liters of wine a day, starting with a 6 ounce glass of wine with breakfast and continuing at regular intervals throughout the day. The blood alcohol of such a man may range from a low of .02% to about 12%, rarely high enough to cause visible symptoms of intoxication in an experienced drinker.

Thus, although many "inveterate drinkers" may be considered addicted to alcohol, they may go on indefinitely—never really drunk, never completely sober. Unlike the Gamma alcoholic, they usually show no loss of control over their drinking and have no compulsion to drink themselves into a stupor. However, since they often are unable to abstain from alcohol for even a day, they cannot—like so many alcoholics in the United States—"go on the wagon."

The causes of "inveterate drinking" appear, on the whole, more social and economic than psychiatric. The abundance and easy availability of wine and other alcoholic beverages encourages heavy drinking. In Portugal, for instance, a pound of meat costs 11 escudos, a quart of wine 2 escudos.[1] Both the importance of wine-growing to the economy of the country and pride in the national product also tend to bring about social approval of heavy individual consumption.

But socioeconomic factors are hardly the whole answer. France's next-door neighbor is another large wine-growing country, Italy. Here, too, a sizeable proportion of the population not only earn their living through the production and sale of wine but also consume a good deal of their product. Yet, according to available statistics, the rate of alcoholism in Italy is about one-fifth that of France.

This difference may result from a different attitude toward drinking and drunkenness.[1] The Italian tends to accept the use of alcohol as a

TABLE 2. *Apparent consumption of alcohol as contained in distilled spirits, wine and beer in certain countries of the population aged 15 years and over (last available year in each country)*

COUNTRY	YEAR	LITERS PER CAPITA	COUNTRY	YEAR	LITERS PER CAPITA
France	1955	25.72	United Kingdom	1960	6.16
Italy	1960	13.26	Poland	1959	5.58
Switzerland	1950-55	10.85	Denmark	1959	5.57
Australia	1960-61	9.66	Sweden	1959	4.98
New Zealand	1960	9.03	Germany (East)	1960	4.60
Germany (West)	1960	8.84	Ireland	1959	4.15
Belgium	1960	8.48	Israel	1959	3.68
USA	1962	7.99	Norway	1960	3.45
Canada	1961	7.23	Finland	1960	3.33
Hungary	1954	7.00	Netherlands	1958	3.19
Peru	1957	6.55			

NOTES: Calculations for this table are based on the best available information from each country, although it should be noted that they are "apparent" rather than actual, since they are derived from such available information as the amount of tax-paid wine delivered to distributors and other indirect data. Only countries with adequate statistics not more than 10 years old have been included.

Comparisons are of dubious legitimacy when the time is not the same. Also of dubious validity is the use of the same population base (whether total, age 15 and over, or any other) for all countries, since the true proportion of drinkers is different in various countries. Only the per capita consumption of actual drinkers would give the most satisfactory comparison.

(*From* Efron, V., and Keller, M.: Selected Statistical Tables on the Consumption of Alcohol, 1850-1962, and on Alcoholism, 1930-1960, New Brunswick, Rutgers Center of Alcohol Studies, 1963, p. 10.)

food, to be taken in moderation and with meals. Though he may drink as much as a liter of wine a day, he probably will drink only with his noon and evening meals. Moreover, there is no social pressure to drink in Italy. Unlike the Frenchman—who often considers heavy drinking a proof of manhood [3]—the Italian will accept the abstainer's refusal without comment. Even more important, in Italy there are definite disapproval of more than moderate drinking and severe and consistent social sanctions against intoxication that are lacking in France. Concerned about the number of "inveterate drinkers," both the government and private citizens of France are striving to remedy the situation. The Council on Alcoholism and such voluntary agencies as Comité National de Défense Contre l'Alcoolisme concentrate primarily on preventive education, as well as the collection and dissemination of data on alcoholism.

RUSSIA–DISPENSARIES AND "DUTCH UNCLE" TALKS

The Russians, traditionally a hard-drinking people, have a capacity for vodka that many Western visitors find truly awe-inspiring. During the days of the Tsars, at any rate, one Russian writer described conditions:

And through the village there sounded the desperate howl of the wife: "The man drinks!" And there rose up a tremendous, monstrous drinking seen nowhere else on God's earth, and it moved all across the Russian land, provoking drunkenness in all—in some, quiet, broken, sad; in others, wild and spirited. The Kabaks [taverns] caused drunkenness, drunkenness caused zapoi [the drinking without letting up, alcoholism], and for zapoi treatment was needed. . . .[4]

According to the present Russian government, however, zapoi is no longer the serious problem it was in prerevolutionary days, when about a third of all beds in mental hospitals were occupied by alcoholics. Professor Rapoport,[5] speaking at the Moscow Ministry of Health, reported that by 1953 only about 2% of these beds were filled by alcoholics. Since 1950, about five or six persons per 10,000 of population have been applying for treatment of alcoholism each year.

Treatment for the majority of alcoholics is given mostly in dispensaries; and methods include psychotherapy, individual and group hypnosis, various drugs, occupational therapy, and aversion treatment.[5, 6] The Russian's psychotherapy, however, is usually different from that of the Western world and appears to be closer to office counseling or "Dutch uncle" talks.[5] Professor Rapoport believes that this man-to-man talk is the best tool in dealing with alcoholics.

On the whole, these methods of treatment are not unlike those in America. There appears to be more stress, though, on various forms of conditioned-reflex therapy, not too surprising since such methods are based on the classic conditioning studies of Pavlov. The Russians, in fact, were the first to issue a scientific report on the value of using this technic in the treatment of alcoholism.

In conditioned-reflex therapy—employed in this country as well—the physician generally gives the alcoholic patient a short-acting emetic drug, such as apomorphine, waits five to ten minutes until the patient begins reacting to the drug, then lets him drink his favorite alcoholic beverage. Donald Hammersley described a typical session: "As a strong wave of nausea developed, and before actual vomiting began, the patient was given one and one-half oz. of whiskey and told to swallow it. . . . If the administration of whiskey was properly timed, emesis occurred in less than thirty seconds after ingestion of whiskey." [7] Following several highly unpleasant treatments of this nature, the patient, understandably enough, is conditioned to become nauseated at the sight of alcohol, to vomit at the first few mouthfuls. The system has flaws of course: the strong resistance of many alcoholics to the whole procedure, the need for almost continuous medical supervision, and the gradual "deconditioning" of the alcoholic in the weeks following cessation of treatment.

A somewhat less painful version of this method is hypnotherapy, also popular in the Soviet Union. During hypnosis, reports Professor I. Strelchuk,[8] the patient is exposed to the odor of an alcoholic beverage and given some to drink. At the same time, he is told that he not only has lost his desire for alcohol, but that even the odor or taste of it will, in the future, be highly unpleasant and provoke nausea, severe headache and dizziness. Such hypnotic suggestions, repeated every two or three days, eventually lead to a stable dislike for alcohol that may, in the majority of patients, last from four to six months.

In patients with what Professor Strelchuk calls a "pseudo withdrawal syndrome," characterized by an irritable-depressed psychic mood and an intense desire for alcohol, prolonged sleep therapy has proved quite effective. The patient is kept asleep, by a combination of hypnosis and hypnotic drugs, for 18 to 22 hours out of every 24 and is fed intravenously. When he awakes, five to ten days later, the pseudo-withdrawal syndrome presumably has had a chance to wear itself out.

While the Soviet medical men specializing in alcoholism hold views concerning causes and treatment similar to those of our own specialists, the general Soviet physician and psychiatrist, according to Dr. Morris Chafetz,[9] who studied the problem firsthand in Iron Curtain countries, consider the alcoholic patient a delinquent and avoid treating him unless a medical complication is present. This attitude, Dr. Chafetz points out, is not uncommon in the United States: on the whole, "the Soviet attitude toward the alcoholic patient tends to be moralistic and punitive, as in the United States."

A "TOTAL APPROACH" TO ALCOHOLISM

Czechoslovakia is one of the few Iron Curtain countries in which alcoholism statistics can be obtained. These suggest that alcoholics make up roughly 2% of the population (versus about 3% of the population in the United States). According to Dr. Chafetz,[9] the Czechs, although they have fewer personnel than we have, in some cases have better facilities for dealing with the alcoholic. In addition, they have various treatment programs worthy of our study. One innovation is the antialcoholic station to which the police bring intoxicated persons for "drying-out service." These stations, staffed principally by male nurses and by psychiatrists specializing in the treatment of alcoholism, not only provide medical treatment for acute alcoholic states but also serve as alcoholic detection centers. On his discharge from the station, the patient's name is given to the district alcoholic center, and he must report to this center for a lecture on alcoholism. In addition, a district doctor is sent to call on him to determine whether he is, or is not, an alcoholic. If the medical verdict is yes—or if the individual is seen at an antialcoholic station a second time—a psychiatrist is called in and long-term treatment initiated.

Treatment of chronic alcoholism is usually conducted at an antialcoholic clinic and consists of individual and group therapy, often for the patient's mate as well, and disulfiram treatment. If these measures prove ineffective, the alcoholic is institutionalized for more intensive treatment. For instance, at the Apolinar, the main center of antialcoholic activities in Prague, an example of the Czech's "total approach" can be seen. The program stresses physical and mental rehabilitation and, in the words of a socialist physician, "is concerned to attract the attention of the patient from his own narrow, individual interests to the interests of a small community (roommates, family), a larger community (all patients in the department, people in the work place) and the whole community (society)." [9]

The three-month program includes psychotherapy, work treatment and educational activities. One interesting idea is that of giving long-term abstainers particular recognition, encouraging them to help other alcoholics, even allowing them to work in alcoholism clinics as part of the clinic personnel. Abstainers who are actors and artists come to perform before alcoholic patients, thus helping in the "identification process," which the Czechs consider highly useful in helping the alcoholic maintain and create new self-respect.

REFERENCES CHAPTER 5

1. Jellinek, E. M.: The Disease Concept of Alcoholism, New Haven, Hill House Press, 1960.

2. Bastide, H.: Population 9:13, 1954.

3. Sadoun, R., and Lolli, G.: Quart J Stud Alcohol 23:449, 1962.

4. Efron, V.: Quart J Stud Alcohol 16:484, 1955.

5. Scope Weekly 2:10 (2), 1957.

6. Efron, V.: Quart J Stud Alcohol 19:668, 1958.

7. Hammersley, D. W.: *in* Wallerstein, R. S., ed.: Hospital Treatment of Alcoholism, New York, Basic, 1957.

8. Medical Tribune 3:2 (14), 1962.

9. Chafetz, M. E.: New Eng J Med 265:68, 1961.

CHAPTER 6

ALCOHOLISM—18TH CENTURY AND TODAY

THE BELIEF that so potent a liquid as alcohol must be capable of causing serious disease is an old one. Benjamin Rush,[1] in his famous *Inquiry into the Effects of Ardent Spirits upon the Human Body and Mind,* assured his readers that "ardent spirits" dispose the body "to every form of acute disease; they moreover excite fevers in persons predisposed to them, from other causes." Among the diseases which "are the usual consequences of the habitual use of ardent spirits," Rush listed:

1. A decay of appetite, sickness at stomach, and a puking of bile or a discharge of a frothy and viscid phlegm by hawking, in the morning;
2. Obstructions of the liver. . . .
3. Jaundice and dropsy of the belly and limbs, and finally of every cavity in the body. . . .
4. Hoarseness, and a husky cough, which often terminate in consumption and sometimes in an acute and fatal disease of the lungs.
5. Diabetes, that is, a frequent and weakening discharge of pale, or sweetish urine.
6. Redness, and eruptions on different parts of the body. They generally begin on the nose, after gradually extending all over the face, sometimes extend to the limbs in the form of leprosy. They have been called 'Rumbuds' when they appear in the face. . . .
7. A fetid breath, composed of every thing, that is offensive in putrid animal matter.
8. Frequent and disgusting belchings. . . .
9. Epilepsy.
10. Gout, in all its various forms of swelled limbs, colic, palsy and apoplexy. Lastly,
11. Madness. . . .

Today, 150 years later, many laymen would probably still consider this a reasonably accurate, although overwrought, picture of alcohol's destructive powers; and they could point to a sufficient number of individuals, "shattered" in mind or body, to back up their views.

Twentieth-century research, however, while it hardly establishes alcohol as a benign and milklike beverage, tends to soften its image somewhat. Alcohol is indeed implicated in a number of varied diseases, but its role in most cases appears to be an *indirect* one. "The net effect of a brief survey of some of the fairly numerous conditions popularly and clinically associated with alcoholism," according to E. E. Lape,[2] "is to deprive alcohol of a direct causal role and to focus attention on the general malnutrition, specific nutritional deficiencies, the metabolic derangements in psychoses, neuropathies, pellagra, liver cirrhosis and other pathological conditions frequently found in alcoholics—but not peculiar to them."

ALCOHOL'S MORE DIRECT EFFECTS

Alcohol's chief pharmacologic action is on the central nervous system, where it acts as a depressant, slowing and hampering both motor performance, such as the control of speech and eye movements, and mental function.

Alcoholic intoxication—"singing, hallooing, roaring. . . ." Drunkenness is easily the most common clinical manifestation of alcoholism, and its psychological and physical effects have been recorded by countless observers. One of the most graphic descriptions of the intoxicated individual was sketched by Rush.[1] Among the symptoms which characterize the drunkard, he noted:

Certain extravagant acts which indicate a temporary fit of madness. These are singing, hallooing, roaring, imitating the noises of brute animals, jumping, tearing off clothes, dancing naked, breaking glasses and china, and dashing other articles of household furniture upon the ground or floor.

After a while the paroxysm of drunkenness is completely formed. The face now becomes flushed, the eyes project, and are somewhat watery, winking is less frequent than is natural; the under lip is protruded—the head inclines a little to one shoulder;—the jaw falls;—belchings and hickup (sic) take place—the limbs totter;—the whole body staggers. The unfortunate subject of this history next falls on his seat,—he looks around him with a vacant countenance, and mutters inarticulate sounds to himself;—he attempts to rise and walk. In this attempt, he falls upon his side, from which he gradually turns upon his back.

He now closes his eyes, and falls into a profound sleep, frequently attended by snoring, and profuse sweats, and sometimes with such a relaxation of the muscles which confine the bladder and the lower bowels, as to produce a

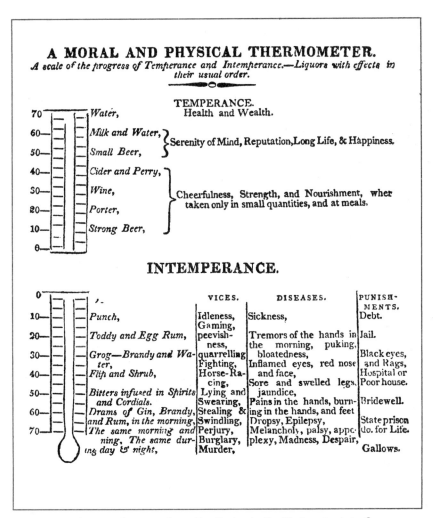

Fig. 2. Reproduction of a page from Dr. Benjamin Rush's *Inquiry into the Effects of Ardent Spirits upon the Human Body and Mind.*

symptom which delicacy forbids me to mention. In this condition, he often lies from ten, twelve, and twenty-four hours, to two, three, and four and five days, an object of pity and disgust to his family and friends. . . .

Since the signs of intoxication are distinctive, to say the least, they generally present no problem in diagnosis. Coma, of course, is the one exception; diagnosis of alcoholic coma can never be safely made merely on the basis of a flushed face, stupor, and the odor of alcohol, but only after the careful exclusion of other causes.[3] Almost all the signs of intoxication result from alcohol's depressant action on nerve cells in certain selected parts of the nervous system, possibly the upper brain-stem and diencephalon, in a manner similar to that of the barbiturates or inhalant anesthesia. Unlike the general anesthetics, however, the safety margin is narrow, and the ingestion of too much alcohol can cause the irreversible depression of respiration that accounts for the occasional coma fatality.[3]

Abstinence withdrawal syndrome—"tremulous, hallucinatory, convulsive, delirious." When the alcoholic has stopped drinking for a while, he is subject to a second constellation of symptoms. These, too, the sharp-eyed Dr. Rush [1] has set down.

His recovery from this fit of intoxication is marked with several peculiar appearances. He opens his eyes, and closes them again;—he gapes and stretches his limbs—he then coughs and pukes;—his voice is hoarse,—he rises with difficulty, and staggers to a chair; his eyes resemble balls of fire,—his hands tremble,—he loathes the sight of food;—he calls for a glass of spirits to compose his stomach—now and then he emits a deep-fetched sigh, or groan, from a transient twinge of conscience, but he more frequently scolds, and curses every thing around him. In this state of languor and stupidity, he remains for two or three days, before he is able to resume his former habits of business and conversation.

This time, Dr. Rush understated his case. The alcoholic seen most often by physicians—particularly by hospital staffs—is often in an even worse condition. Morrison, describing a group of 168 alcoholics hospitalized in his alcoholism clinic, noted that many were acutely ill on admission:

They were nervous, tremulous, weak, and many had abdominal pains with nausea and vomiting. Most were dehydrated as shown by increased blood hematocrit indicative of hemoconcentration. Practically all complained of insomnia. On physical examination, most patients had gross tremors of the extremities, injected eyes, and flushed faces. Disorders other than alcoholism including diabetes mellitus, psychosis, fracture, cirrhosis, gouty arthritis, and others were encountered in 12 patients.[4]

According to Victor and Adams,[3] "the shakes"—a state of tremulousness often combined with general irritability, nausea and vomiting—is the most frequent cause for admission of an alcoholic to the hospital. Delirium tremens is apparently a severer form of the same condition, with even more intense psychomotor and speech overactivity, autonomic overactivity (sweating, tachycardia, dilated pupils and fever), more profound disorders of perception (resulting in auditory and visual hallucinations) and greater confusion. Distinctly a serious illness, it has a mortality rate of 15% in these investigators' experience. Death frequently occurs because of the complications of trauma and infections or, more directly, because of peripheral circulatory collapse or hyperthermia.

At first glance, both the acute alcoholic episode and the withdrawal phase would seem to result from the toxic effects of alcohol. The symptoms of toxicity, however—slurred speech, staggering, stupor—are quite different from the symptom complex of tremor, hallucinosis, and delirium. The first state is associated with a high level of alcohol in the blood, the second with a low or negligible level. Perhaps most significant, continued use of alcohol not only intensifies the symptoms of intoxication but can actually nullify symptoms such as nausea, vomiting and tremor. Based on their own studies and those of Isbell,[5] Victor and Adams postulate that, in the chronic alcoholic, the neurologic symptoms of withdrawal "are the result of excessive and disorganized activity of those parts of the central nervous system normally acted upon by alcohol, after the diminution in the levels of blood alcohol, *viz.,* after sleep or enforced abstinence."

MANAGEMENT OF THE WITHDRAWAL PHASE

Just as the signs of intoxication and withdrawal usually present little problem in differential diagnosis, the management of these conditions also follows well-known patterns. They are, however, a far cry from the patterns recognized in Rush's day. Among other "remedies" for a fit of drunkenness, Rush suggested thrusting a feather down the patient's throat to induce vomiting, plunging him into cold water, terrifying him into sobriety, provoking "profuse sweats" in him or even severely whipping him in order to excite "a revulsion of the blood from the brain, to the external parts of the body."

The distressing withdrawal symptoms demand expert medical attention, often in a hospital setting. Typical treatment given to patients in an alcoholic clinic was outlined by Morrison in a recently published study.[4] At the time of admission, all patients routinely received one of the newer psychopharmaceuticals either intramuscularly or orally. Adjusted doses of the agent were administered throughout the patient's stay. In addition, all received "two daily intravenous injections of 1,000 cc of 10% fructose in water plus liberal quantities of fruit juice to correct dehydration, 12 units of regular insulin to hasten the metabolism of alcohol, and 2 cc of vitamin B complex intramuscularly to combat avitaminosis." In three cases, ACTH was administered concurrently for the control of alcoholic hallucinosis.

On this regimen, response was good in all but five of 168 patients. The psychopharmaceutical's value was stressed, since it "gave marked relief of anxiety, tension and tremor in many patients, and . . . relieved one of the most distressing of all symptoms for these patients—inability to sleep." The agent used in this study, chlordiazepoxide HCl (Librium), was found particularly useful because it not only prevented withdrawal convulsions in all patients but also, by providing a favorable mental outlook, "seemed to counteract the morbid anesthetic depression so often produced by the continued use of alcohol."

REFERENCES CHAPTER 6

1. Rush, B.: Inquiry into the Effects of Ardent Spirits upon the Human Body and Mind, *in* Brookfield, E. Merriam, ed. 8, 1814, reprinted in Quart J Stud Alcohol 4:321, 1943.

2. Lape, E. E., ed.: Medical Research, A Midcentury Survey, vol. 2, Boston, Little, 1955, p. 537.

3. Victor, M., and Adams, R. D.: Amer J Clin Nutr 9:379, 1961.

4. Morrison, J. M.: Dis Nerv Syst 24:430, 1963.

5. Isbell, H., *et al.:* Quart J Stud Alcohol 16:1, 1955.

CHAPTER 7

THE PROBLEM DRINKER IN INDUSTRY

O F THE ESTIMATED two million alcoholics currently working in American businesses and industries,[1] the great majority, surprisingly enough, go unrecognized. Because the alcoholic employee is usually in the early or middle stage of this disease, he lacks the dramatic symptoms of later, severe phases. Moreover, even after his domestic and social life have begun to deteriorate, the typical problem drinker makes an enormous effort to protect his job by covering up whatever symptoms he does have.[2] As a result, the problem drinker in industry can, and often does, remain "hidden" for many years.

THE "WORKING" ALCOHOLIC

Although certain industries and professions are popularly associated with "hard drinking," problem drinkers appear to have jobs in all industries and at all occupational levels. As the vice-president of one large firm observed, he and his colleagues were impressed by the apparently widespread occurrence of alcoholism throughout the employee force. "It was found among our craftsmen," he noted, "our line crews, our foremen, and our clerks. It occurred in our middle levels of management and occasionally in the higher management group. It also occurred among our women, although with less frequency than among our men." [3] Problem drinkers do tend to concentrate in one age group—35 to 50 [1]—and that this period represents an individual's prime productive years is one reason that alcoholism is so vital a personnel problem.

Fortunately, for treatment, only a minority of "working" alcoholics appear to be deeply neurotic or psychotic. Most have emotional problems, of course, and many may also have a physiologic sensitivity to alcohol. But several investigators suggest that, for the relatively stable employed alcoholic, social influences probably play the most important etiologic role. Franco, in fact, estimates that nearly 80% of these employees are nonaddictive alcoholics whose condition stems primarily from social situations.[4]

At all occupational levels, social pressures can often almost compel an individual to drink. Particularly for men, drinking is usually considered a sign of good fellowship and even of virility. In some situations, employees seriously believe that the performance of their duties *requires* the liberal use of alcohol. Trice [1] cites such examples as a bond salesman who was convinced that his sales volume would decline if he did not drink with his customers; a construction foreman who felt that he had to drink steadily throughout the day to cope effectively with his tough workmen; and a sales executive who believed that he could better handle both subordinates and clients if he drank heavily with them.

The susceptible individual who starts to drink in response to social custom usually experiences a sharp improvement in his feeling of well-being whenever he drinks. As he gradually builds up a tolerance to alcohol, however, he must keep increasing his intake in order to maintain this feeling. Quite often, he becomes extremely sensitive about his increasing "need" for alcohol and resents any reference to it; indeed, Trice [1] suggests that an exterior of cockiness, excessive independence and superiority often masks a hypersensitivity to criticism.

Persistent remorse and guilt about his excessive drinking create a nagging, constant tension. The problem drinker reduces this by more alcohol—and a vicious cycle begins: he drinks excessively, hates himself for it, sets up desperate regulations to control the amount of alcohol he will consume, fails to keep the regulations, and drinks even more because of his guilt and self-hate.

EARLY IDENTIFICATION OF THE PROBLEM DRINKER

Except for his family and drinking companions, few may realize the developing alcoholic's problem. Most of the early signs of excessive drinking—the memory blackouts, the constant preoccupation with alcohol, the increasing tolerance for it—can be hidden from supervisors, employers, even co-workers. The developing alcoholic, too often, is considered by others as "a good worker who drinks too much now and then," rather than as an individual in the early stages of illness. In order to identify the alcoholic at the earliest possible stage, Maxwell [2] undertook an investigation of the kind of drinking signs which appear

TABLE 3. *On-the-job drinking signs ranked by % of respondents indicating serious or moderate occurrence* [2]

SIGNS	DEGREE OF OCCURRENCE		
* Among first drinking signs to appear	Serious/ Moderate	Rare/ Mild	Never
1. Hangovers on the job *	84%	12%	4%
2. Increased nervousness/jitteriness *	83	14	3
3. More edgy/irritable	75	16	9
4. Putting things off	72	16	12
5. Red or bleary eyes	70	20	10
6. Less even, more spasmodic work pace	69	18	13
7. Sensitive to opinions about your drinking	68	19	13
8. Hand tremors *	68	22	10
9. Avoiding boss or associates	67	18	15
10. Neglected details formerly attended to	66	22	12
11. Indignant when your drinking was mentioned	66	20	14
12. Drinking at lunch time *	61	17	22
13. Morning drinking before work *	61	18	21
14. Flushed face	61	23	16
15. Lower quantity of work	60	23	16
16. Using "breath purifiers"	59	20	21
17. Making mistakes or errors of judgment	58	34	8
18. Lower quality of work	58	23	19
19. Mood changes after lunchtime or other drinking	56	19	25
20. More intolerant of fellow workers	56	22	22
21. More resentful of fellow workers	55	21	24
22. More unusual excuses for absences	54	24	22
23. More suspicious of fellow workers	53	22	25
24. Absenteeism, half-day or day *	52	35	13
25. Drinking during working hours	50	23	27
26. Increase in *real* minor illnesses	50	28	22
27. More tendency to blame other workers	47	22	31
28. Borrowing money from employer or associates	46	20	34
29. Leaving post temporarily	44	30	26
30. More aggressive toward fellow workers	44	28	28
31. Wanting a different job assignment	40	19	41
32. Leaving work early	39	32	29
33. Longer lunch periods	39	25	36
34. Less neat in dress and appearance	38	23	39
35. Showing up intoxicated	38	32	30
36. Loud talking	37	25	38
37. Swelling of the face	37	23	50
38. More careful in dress and appearance	33	29	38
39. Late to work	33	33	34
40. Unnecessary long distance calls	20	17	63
41. Lost-time accidents *off* the job	18	24	58
42. Sleeping on the job	15	20	65
43. Minor accidents *on* the job	9	25	66
44. Lost-time accidents *on* the job	5	14	81

on the job first. Over 400 male alcoholics, who had either "recovered" or who were still under treatment, were asked to fill out questionnaires concerning their problem drinking (see Table 3). The subjects were asked to note, in particular, which of 44 drinking signs were among the first to be experienced and which proved to be fairly serious and frequently occurring symptoms.

From this table, a portrait of the "working" alcoholic emerges. In all probability, he is suffering from a hangover (over 90% of the respondents reported this symptom). This means he is trying to perform his assigned tasks while fighting a combination of thirst, headache, fatigue, jitters and nausea. Incessant and abnormal thirst probably forces him to make repeated visits to the water fountain and the rest room. He will undoubtedly gulp aspirin tablets in an attempt to allay his severe headache, and drink as much black coffee as possible in order to counteract overwhelming fatigue. If these measures fail to bring relief, he begins to manage his hangover with more alcohol. A morning drink becomes routine, as drinking at lunch time does. Whether he risks drinking during the rest of the work day, his guilt, nervousness and physical discomfort make him irritable, difficult to get along with, and less efficient.

While absenteeism is one of the fairly early drinking signs, the employed problem drinker, trying to hold on to his job, apparently makes serious efforts to avoid its repeated occurrence. Maxwell suggests that morning drinking may be a means not merely of handling a hangover but also of avoiding absence. Drinking on the job, oddly enough, may be considered another means of avoiding excessive absences, although it often means more "partial absences" as the suffering worker leaves his post to get a drink, prolongs his lunch hour, or leaves the job early. Some of the absences that do occur may be only indirectly due to drinking. That the alcoholic often substitutes drinking for eating makes him particularly susceptible to minor illnesses, such as colds, stomach upsets and neuritis.[1]

Although it might seem that a good many drinking signs are easily observable—especially such physical and behavioral signs as red or bleary eyes, hand tremor, flushed face, increased jitteriness, or spasmodic work pace—a number of early and even middle-stage alcoholics apparently can hide their problem for years. Asked by Maxwell how long they were able to function on the job after their drinking problem developed, at least half the men questioned reported being able to keep signs of their problem hidden for a year or more, 30% for 3 years or more, 22% for 5 years or more. Asked how soon they sought help for their problem, 6% of the men said they sought help within a year, 12% within 1 to 2 years, 16% within 3 to 4 years, 30% within 5 to 9 years, 18% within 10 to 14 years, 11% within 15 to 19 years, and 7% within 20 to 32 years. About half the men reported seven or more years of problem drinking before seeking help.

WHAT INDUSTRY IS DOING

In the past two decades, more and more businesses and industries have stopped thinking of alcoholism as a disciplinary problem and have adopted a treatment-oriented approach to problem-drinking employees. Consolidated Edison of New York, for instance, officially recognized chronic alcoholism as a medical condition in 1947 and formulated a "Company Procedure on Alcoholism," which aimed for early recognition of the problem drinker, rehabilitation if possible, and the establishment of a consistent basis for discharging employees if rehabilitation failed.[4,5]

In 1952, Con Edison volunteered to underwrite the cost of a Consultation Clinic for Alcoholism at the NYU–Bellevue Medical Center. The first to be devoted solely to the treatment of alcoholism in industry, this clinic opened on February 4, 1952. At the present time, a number of companies in the New York area utilize the services of this clinic by paying a consultation fee for the initial evaluation of employees suspected of having a drinking problem. If treatment proves necessary, the employee is asked to pay a regular clinic fee. He may, if he prefers, go to his personal physician instead—or simply refuse all treatment and try to solve his drinking problem on his own.

The results of such industrial programs are generally encouraging. Con Edison conducted a follow-up study to evaluate its particular plan. The study revealed that, during the years 1952 to 1955, 183 cases of alcoholism were recognized at Con Edison and, of these, 145 accepted referral to the Consultation Clinic. Of the men who continued treatment at the clinic, 60% were eventually either rehabilitated or "socially recovered" and 30% were considered much improved. The majority of this group were able to maintain their jobs, and absenteeism among the members was reduced from an average of 13.5 days a year to less than 4 days. It was pointed out, however, that the high incidence of recovery may have occurred because the men were "specially selected and specially motivated." The long years of employment of these men—over 20 years at the same company—reflected relative stability and also served as a lever in developing motivation toward treatment, since the probation process placed job security in jeopardy.[5]

The type of program set up by Con Edison—a special clinic for alcoholism separated from the company—is one method of dealing with the problem. Other [1] companies have differing rehabilitation policies. In general, the decision to treat an employee as a problem drinker is made by the company's medical staff, aided in some cases by psychologists and even by AA members who work as nonprofessional members of the medical department. In larger firms, programs usually provide for specific counseling within the company and referral to outside special agencies. In smaller firms, referral may be made to state and municipal clinics or to private facilities. Whatever program is followed, the Medical Director of one company has observed: "The results of rehabilitation attempts are apt to be more successful in industry than in any other segment of the population because it is this group who have the greatest motivation for overcoming the social, financial, and job difficulties into which they have been thrown because of their drinking." [6]

REFERENCES CHAPTER 7

1. Trice, H. M.: The Problem Drinker on the Job, Ithaca, NY State School of Industrial and Labor Relations, Cornell Univ, 1959.
2. Maxwell, M. A.: Quart J Stud Alcohol 21:655, 1960.
3. Ferrier, D. W.: Management Policy and the Alcoholic, Ottawa, Oct 31, 1953.
4. Franco, S. C.: Industr Med Surg 26:221, 1957.
5. Pfeffer, A. Z.: Alcoholism, New York, Grune, 1958.
6. Wilkins, G. F.: Industr Med Surg 22:33, 1953.

CHAPTER 8

MEDICAL COMPLICATIONS OF ALCOHOL

THE DIRE EFFECTS of alcohol on man were once dramatically, if not inaccurately, driven home by temperance leaders with a simple "experiment." Neatly breaking a fresh egg into a glass of straight whiskey, they pointed to "the grey matter of the brain" (the albumen of the egg) coagulating and shriveling horribly before the audience's eyes.

More conservative experiments and a vast number of physiologic studies have been able to trace surprisingly few of the "complications" of alcoholism directly to the compound itself. While an overdose may lead to fatal coma, and the syndrome of acute alcoholism as well as the DTs of the chronic alcoholic are usually appallingly clear, it has proved difficult to establish definite cause-and-effect relationships between ethyl alcohol and most disorders associated with chronic drinking. In most cases, the problem is complicated by nutritional deficiencies of various kinds, psychic factors, or even the presence of higher congeners in the alcoholic drinks imbibed.

GASTROINTESTINAL COMPLICATIONS

One of the most common conditions due directly to chronic over-indulgence in alcohol is gastritis. When the drinks consumed contain 20% of alcohol or more, gastric secretion tends to be inhibited and peptic activity depressed. Concentrations of over 40% are quite irritating to the mucosa and cause congestive hyperemia and inflammation. In chronic alcoholism, the mucous membrane goes through successive stages of glandular destruction, erosion, formation of cysts, destruction of the muscularis mucosae. Symptoms may be indistinguishable from those of peptic ulcer, carcinoma or functional distress, and differential diagnosis may require gastroscopic inspection of the mucosa, which shows localized, irregular and ragged hypertrophied inelastic folds.

In contrast to the direct, clearly irritating role of alcohol in gastritis, its place as an etiologic factor in cirrhosis is uncertain. Although there is certainly a connection—more than 50% of all cases of Laennec's cirrhosis in this country are associated with alcoholism—the nutritional deficiencies commonly occurring in heavy-drinking patients are thought by some to play a major role. This view is supported by experimental studies showing that: 1. cirrhosis can be produced in the laboratory animal by certain protein deficient diets, 2. feeding of choline or methionine protects against cirrhosis, and 3. feeding diets rich in protein favors repair and regeneration of the damaged liver. Probably the consensus favors the view that both alcoholism and nutritional deficiencies contribute to the etiology of cirrhosis.

Indications of cirrhosis are significant weight loss, anorexia, nausea and vomiting, followed by abdominal fullness due at first to flatulence. But since no pain or even unexpected discomfort is experienced at this stage, the condition may go undetected; in about a third of the cases seen at autopsy, it has been latent or unsuspected. The relative significance of other symptoms and signs that may develop gradually with continued neglect are indicated in the accompanying table.

TABLE 4. *Symptoms and signs of advanced Laennec's cirrhosis (% incidence)*
(*Adapted from A. J. Patek, Jr.*[4])

SYMPTOMS	A/124 CASES [*]	B/200 CASES [†]	SIGNS (*cont'd*)	A/124 CASES [*]	B/200 CASES [†]
Weight loss	89%	58%	Edema	69	58
Nausea and vomiting	51	30	Jaundice	67	45
Abdominal pain	50	46	Vascular spiders	62	..
Epistaxis	40	..	Dilated veins	61	34
Hematemesis	34	13	Palpable spleen	55	32
			Fever	49	..
SIGNS			Abdominal hernia	33	..
Ascites	93%	100%	Clubbed fingers	18	..
Palpable liver	79	55	Hydrothorax	17	..

[*] *Series included 15 cases of postnecrotic cirrhosis.* [†] *Series included only cases with ascites.*

Thompson [1] strongly advises against relying on hepatic function tests in the diagnosis of early cirrhosis.

More attention should be paid to the mild and varied symptoms of patients, such as loss of weight, lassitude, easy fatigue, dyspepsia, anorexia, nausea, and vomiting; sensations of heaviness with distention after meals and gaseous eructations; bowel irregularities, constipation alternating with diarrhea; bleeding phenomena such as epistaxis, purpura, bleeding gums, hemorrhoids, menorrhagia, and metrorrhagia; diffuse abdominal pain is not uncommon. A more detailed inventory should be made of dietary habits when the physician considers the diagnoses alcoholism and cirrhosis.

A condition found in most alcoholics who reach hospitalization is fatty hepatosis, considered due to the combined effects of excessive alcohol intake and malnutrition. This is readily reversible. In contrast, the relatively rare Mallory-Weiss syndrome may terminate fatally. This consists of profound gastrointestinal hemorrhage caused by lacerations at the cardiac orifice of the stomach, produced by protracted retching and vomiting. Of course, in the presence of esophageal varices secondary to Laennec's cirrhosis, to distinguish hemorrhage due to the varices from esophageal laceration is difficult.

Though many causes of pancreatitis have been suggested and its etiology is still obscure, its high incidence in alcoholics and its occurrence during or shortly after alcoholic sprees make many consider alcohol a frequent factor. The mechanism is uncertain. Pancreatitis also offers considerable problems in differential diagnosis, since the major symptoms of severe epigastric pain, frequently radiating to the back, with nausea and vomiting, may also suggest perforated peptic ulcer, peritonitis, biliary colic, intestinal obstruction, mesenteric thrombosis, coronary occlusion, dissecting aneurysm, and intraabdominal apoplexy. Furthermore, in the early stages, such tests as determination of serum amylase, lipase, bilirubin and blood sugar show significant elevations only during the acute episodes. In most cases, attacks of pain occur five or more years before the diagnosis is established.[6]

NEUROPSYCHIATRIC COMPLICATIONS

The psychic effects of "social drinking" are so readily recognizable that it is to be expected that prolonged indulgence might bring about a number of changes in the central nervous system. The immediate and temporary effects are bolstering; a favorite textbook description is that of Horace [2]:

"What wonders does not wine! It discloses secrets; ratifies and confirms our hopes; thrusts the coward forth to battle; eases the anxious mind of its burden; instructs in arts. Whom has not a cheerful glass made eloquent! Whom not quite free and easy from pinching poverty!"

But since these pleasant effects stem from the depression of higher mental processes that control discrimination, memory, concentration and insight, it is almost predictable that these very faculties would be permanently impaired by chronic excessive intake. Typically, prolonged overindulgence leads to such mental changes as increased irritability and emotional lability, deterioration of work performance and personal habits, lowering of moral standards and dulling of intellect.

However, the diagnosable neuropsychiatric syndromes associated with alcoholism have been quite clearly defined as stemming primarily from the nutritional deficiency so prevalent in alcoholics. Peripheral neuropathies usually develop slowly, first affecting the lower extremities, with pains and paresthesias in the feet and hands, and later, foot drop and wrist drop, and impairment or loss of sensation. Eventually, the deep reflexes of the knees, ankles and arms may weaken or be lost. Both animal and clinical experimentation has led to the conclusion that these proceedings are due to vitamin B deficiencies, especially lack of thiamine.

Severe thiamine deficiency may lead to Wernicke's syndrome, which, although it must develop from long deprivation, usually is sudden in onset. The characteristic picture includes varying degrees of ophthalmoplegia—of vital diagnostic importance—ataxia, mental confusion with clouding of consciousness, and polyneuropathy. The nutritional etiology of this disease is well established through numerous observations, including the fact that outbreaks have occurred in prisoner-of-war camps, and most of the symptoms are rapidly reversible on administration of intravenous thiamine hydrochloride and polyvitamin therapy. The mental clouding and memory defect, however, usually persist, suggesting permanent structural changes.

Patients who recover from Wernicke's syndrome often develop Korsakoff's psychosis. Although the mental changes are more severe and varied, the overlapping of symptomatology at various stages of the two disorders suggests not only common factors in etiology but possibly different facets of the same disease. The major characteristic of Korsakoff's psychosis is memory defect with confabulation and disorientation. In psychological testing, defects in cognitive functioning are marked, e.g., in concentration, verbal and visual abstraction, visual-motor coordination, and learning ability. The memory defect applies to both old and new material; the patient, often jovial, may try to cover up by piecing isolated facts together. Such patients require hospitalization, with intensive vitamin therapy. Although some may become able to function in society, the memory defects and confusion usually persist, and usually they are capable of performing only routine tasks.

Other disorders characterized by mental and personality deterioration seen in advanced chronic alcoholism, and in which the prognosis is poor, include nicotinic acid deficiency encephalopathy, Marchiafava-Bignani syndrome (corpus callosum demyelinating encephalopathy) and paranoid disorders. In addition, any disease or disorder ascribable to nutritional deficiency, such as skin lesions related to avitaminoses or nutritional amblyopia, may occur in malnourished alcoholics.

MISCELLANEOUS COMPLICATIONS

One of the few conditions in which alcohol can be directly and definitely implicated is susceptibility to trauma—as, for example, in drunken driving. While psychic and other factors may also be involved, there can be no doubt that the effect of alcohol on judgment, reaction time and other requisites of safe driving plays an important part in our shocking highway accident rate.

And, finally, alcoholics are subject, of course, to all the other ills to which mankind is liable. Even when there is no direct connection to alcohol itself or related nutritional diseases, the abnormal living habits usually adopted by the habitual heavy drinker can aggravate symptoms.

REFERENCES CHAPTER 8

1. Thompson, G. N., ed.: Alcoholism, Springfield (Ill.), Thomas, 1956.
2. Harrison, T. R., ed.: Principles of Internal Medicine, ed. 4, New York, McGraw-Hill, 1962.
3. Goodman, L. S., and Gilman, A., eds.: The Pharmacological Basis of Therapeutics, ed. 2, New York, Macmillan, 1955.
4. Patek, A. J., Jr.: in Cecil, R. L., and Loeb, R. F., eds.: A Textbook of Medicine, ed. 10, Philadelphia, Saunders, 1959, pp. 880 ff.
5. Wortis, S. B.: ibid., pp. 1620 ff.
6. Wollaeger, E. E.: ibid., pp. 908 ff.

CHAPTER 9

PREVENTION–KNOTTY PROBLEM

IN ALCOHOLISM, an ounce of prevention is worth a good deal more than many pounds of cure. On the surface, the prevention of alcoholism depends on a single premise: one attempts to keep the "host" away from the "causative agent;" failing that, one tries to keep the "causative agent" away from the "host." To these ends, countless maneuvers have been attempted, among them "restrictive legislation, authoritarian fiat, appeals to intelligence or to spiritual motive, increased retail prices for various beverages, arrests and sentences for drunkenness, revocation of license for driving under the influence, increased taxation on the beverage industry. . . ." [1] But, unfortunately, the net result of these acts of prevention, even when applied with full legal force and fury, has so far been rather negligible.

PERSUASION, THE FIRST WEAPON

Earlier ages also found monumental the task of keeping drinker and alcohol apart until a comparatively short time ago; persuasion—not the most potent of weapons—was almost the only one available in the war against excessive drinking. About 3,000 years ago, an emotional Egyptian wrote what may have been the first temperance tract.

"Take not upon thyself to drink a jug of beer," he pleaded in a work called *Wisdom of Ani*, because if you do, "Thou speakest, and an unintelligible utterance issueth from thy mouth. If thou fallest down and thy limbs break, there is none to hold out a hand to thee. Thy companions in drink stand up and say: 'Away with this sot.' If there then cometh one to seek thee in order to question thee, thou art found lying on the ground, and thou art like a little child." [2]

Whether this depressing portrait had much effect on Egyptian prob-

lem drinkers is not known. But in the *Shu Ching,* written about 650
B.C., the Chinese advice to potential alcohol misusers starts out by ad-
mitting "Men will not do without *kiu* [a form of beer]. To prohibit it
and secure total abstinence from it is beyond the power even of sages.
Here, therefore, we have warnings on the abuse of it." The warnings,
recommending moderation, are fairly well summed up by the often
quoted Japanese proverb: "At the first cup, man drinks wine. At the
second cup, wine drinks wine. At the third cup, wine drinks man." [2]

The Bible denounces the misuse of alcohol.[3]

> Woe unto them that rise up early in the morning, that they may follow
> strong drink; that continue until night, till wine inflame them!
> Woe unto them that are mighty to drink wine . . .(Isaiah 5:11,22).
> Wine is a mocker, strong drink is raging: and whoso is deceived thereby
> is not wise (Proverbs 20:1).
> At the last it biteth like a serpent, and stingeth like an adder (Proverbs
> 23:32).

But it savors its proper uses. "Wine maketh glad the heart of man," the
psalmist sings (Psalms 104:15), and King Lemuel's mother makes a
nice distinction for its use:

> It is not for kings, O Lemuel, it is not for kings to drink wine; nor for
> princes strong drink:
> Lest they drink, and forget the law, and pervert the judgment of any of
> the afflicted.
> Give strong drink unto him that is ready to perish, and wine unto those
> that be of heavy hearts.
> Let him drink, and forget his poverty, and remember his misery no more
> (Proverbs 31:4-7).

THE ROCKY ROAD TO PROHIBITION

If the concept of total abstinence was almost entirely absent in
earlier civilizations, it was equally foreign to the colonists who first
came to America from England. For them as for their ancestors, alcohol had religious, medical, dietary and recreational significance. It also
had commercial significance: the manufacture of rum became for a
long time New England's largest industry. In various parts of the new
country, converting corn and other grains into whiskey soon proved to
be the most profitable way of transporting "crops" to market.

The increasing popularity of distilled spirits was one of the factors
that led to the strong "antidrinking" movement in the United States.
Before 1700—when drinking was largely confined to the home, and
beer and wine were the favored drinks—warnings and mild punish-

ment were generally enough to cope with occasional overindulgence. But in the next century or so, drinking patterns changed.[4] Taverns appeared in almost every town, "hard" liquor was soon the common choice, and drunkenness became a problem.

By the 19th century, many physicians and clergymen had joined the growing temperance movement. Previously, alcohol had been widely considered to have medicinal virtues if nothing else. But in the 1830's— following the lead of the famous Dr. Benjamin Rush—medical men were agreeing that alcohol actually served no useful purpose at all; it had no value as a medicine and, moreover, it did not, as commonly believed, increase the working efficiency of farmers and laborers. Clergymen, too, were developing new theories about the use of alcohol. A good many, reexamining the Bible's apparent sanction of moderate drinking, came to a radical new conclusion. When the Bible appeared to sanction the use of wine, they held, it was referring to unfermented grape juice; when it condemned the use of wine, it was referring to the fermented variety.

Thus, the way was clear to advocate total abstinence. And between 1840 and 1860 a number of temperance groups formed—such as the Sons of Temperance and the Independent Order of Good Templars— whose philosophy was opposition no longer to the more than occasional use of "hard" liquor but to the use of alcoholic beverages of any kind and at any time.[1]

RISE AND FALL OF THE 18TH AMENDMENT

To achieve the new goal of total abstinence, legal enforcement seemed to be essential. The strong influence of the Templars made the question of prohibition suddenly an important nationwide political issue, and in 1872, the National Prohibition Party first appeared on the ticket with its platform: "Complete Suppression of the Trade in Intoxicating Liquors." Two years later, the Women's Christian Temperance Union was formed to aid in the fight for total abstinence, declaring its purpose "to educate the young; to form a better public sentiment; to reform so far as possible, by religious, ethical and scientific means, the drinking classes; to seek the transforming power of divine grace for ourselves and for all for whom we work." And the most influential and highly organized temperance group of all, the Anti-Saloon League, came into being in 1895. Its members pledged, through "Education, Legislation and Law Enforcement," to eliminate drinking in the United States.[1]

Conditions during the first two decades of the 20th century were ideal for the temperance groups' purpose. A rapid increase in population—chiefly due to stepped-up immigration—and growing industrialization had led to dramatic and often unfavorable changes in modes of urban living. For practical and humanitarian reasons, the period 1900 to 1919 was one of sweeping social reforms. And since for many humanitarians the problems of the congested cities' new inhabitants could be blamed on alcohol, the desire to "do something for the working classes" reinforced the drive to eliminate their alcohol. By 1919, the concept of prohibition had been publicized for over half a century and had been adopted in various parts of the country. But "local option" clearly had many flaws: temperance leaders were well aware that those who wanted liquor could travel out of their communities to get it. Only nationwide prohibition, they felt, had any chance of stopping the potential alcoholic—and in this year "humanitarian zeal combined with a spiritual motive"[1] led to the passage of the 18th Amendment, which prohibited the manufacture and sale of distilled intoxicating liquors.

In October of 1919, Congress passed the Volstead Act, which provided the machinery for administering and enforcing the 18th Amendment. However, almost from the very start, indifference and even resistance to the enforcement of the law by both officials and private citizens served to render it ineffective. The one essential ingredient for the successful enforcement of a prohibition law was lacking—popular support. In 1933, when it was generally acknowledged that the 18th Amendment had failed, the law was repealed. There was, however, no reason for rejoicing, as one observer noted: "If prohibition laws have not solved the liquor problem, neither has the absence of prohibition laws. The records of the centuries give wets and drys little cause for arrogance and much cause for humility."[5]

OTHER LEGAL APPROACHES TO ALCOHOLISM CONTROLS

After 1933, state legislatures settled down to devising liquor control systems that would, as much as possible, protect the individual from his own weakness. A great variety of legislation has since been passed to control all stages of production, distribution and sale of alcoholic beverages. Although the laws vary among the different states, in general most states have adopted either a monopoly plan, through which a board or commission purchases liquor and sells it through official stores, or a license system, under which a state commission grants licenses to private citizens for the sale of alcoholic beverages. In either system, liquor boards and commissions prohibit sales to minors and intoxicated persons, and make a determined effort to prevent disreputable persons from becoming associated with the liquor industry.[1]

Aside from these areas of agreement, liquor laws differ widely on such matters as zoning, sanitation, labeling, advertising, shipping, serving food with drinks, permits for purchases and the like.[4] Since local option laws are in effect in the majority of the states, many cities and towns in the country are legally "dry." And perhaps the favorite legal measure of all, taxation of the liquor industry, has the virtue of being a reasonably "painless" way of raising taxes, whether it deters liquor purchases or not.

Can strong legislative measures control or at least retard the development of alcoholism? Probably not. Most observers feel that legal controls affect the social drinker much more than they affect the alcoholic.[6] The heavy drinker can—and should—be controlled to some extent by such measures as "drunk driving" laws, particularly when they are reinforced by social pressures and well-thought-out educational programs. But the alcoholic is immune, usually, to both social and legal pressures.

PREVENTION OF PROGRESSION

Since preventing the onset of alcoholism appears to be beyond our powers, *secondary* prevention—early intervention in excessive and pathologic drinking in order to prevent the major consequences of alcoholism [6]—takes on paramount importance. Here, at least, the essential tools already exist. By now, almost all physicians, clergymen, social workers and public health personnel are aware of the warning signs of alcoholism and can diagnose it in the earlier stages.

According to most observers, no individual is a better "secondary preventer" than the family physician. Patients and their families tend to come to him first for help with a drinking problem, although the problem may often be disguised. In addition, changes in drinking habits, usually the first sign of potential trouble, can often be detected during a careful medical history. For this reason, it has been suggested that all physicians include questions about alcohol intake in the course of routine case-taking.[7] When a drinking problem appears to be more than just a possibility, a number of physicians now include a questionnaire, such as that developed by the late Robert V. Seliger, of the

TABLE 5. *Test questions* (From R. V. Seliger [8])

1. Do you require a drink the next morning?
2. Do you prefer to drink alone?
3. Do you lose time from work due to drinking?
4. Is your drinking harming your family in any way?
5. Do you need a drink at a definite time daily?
6. Do you get the inner shakes unless you continue drinking?
7. Has drinking made you irritable?
8. Does it make you careless of your family's welfare?
9. Have you become jealous of your husband or wife since drinking?
10. Has drinking changed your personality?
11. Does it cause you body complaints?
12. Does it make you restless?
13. Does it cause you to have difficulty in sleeping?
14. Has it made you more impulsive?
15. Have you less self-control since drinking?
16. Has your initiative decreased?
17. Has your ambition decreased?
18. Do you lack perseverance in pursuing a goal since drinking?
19. Do you drink to obtain social ease? (in shy, timid, self-conscious individuals)
20. Do you drink for self-encouragement? (in persons with feelings of inferiority)
21. To relieve marked feelings of inadequacy?
22. Has your sexual potency suffered since drinking?
23. Do you show marked dislikes and hatreds?
24. Has your jealousy, in general, increased?
25. Do you show marked moodiness as a result of drinking?
26. Has your efficiency decreased?
27. Has your drinking made you more sensitive?
28. Are you harder to get along with?
29. Do you turn to an inferior environment while drinking?
30. Is drinking endangering your health?
31. It it affecting your peace of mind?
32. Is it making your home life unhappy?
33. Is it jeopardizing your business?
34. Is it clouding your reputation?
35. Is drinking disturbing the harmony of your life?

Johns Hopkins University School of Medicine,[8] to determine how serious the problem may be. In each question, this test deals with a sign that has appeared so consistently in the early records of abnormal drinking that there can be no doubt that it is a danger signal. Aside from the patient himself, it is suggested that the questions be also answered by the patient's mate or a friend.

In the earlier stages of alcoholism, the personal physician can do much to prevent the patient from deteriorating into the chronic phase. "It is important," suggests Brightman, "to make a complete diagnosis of the patient's condition, including a determination of whether addiction is present, the rapidity with which the alcoholic pattern is changing, the relationship of the drinking to underlying mental and physical disorders and the importance of various social or environmental factors."[7] The physician's sympathy and understanding are important concomitants of treatment.

As far as medical treatment itself is concerned, the past few years have seen the development of drugs and technics that have led to greatly increased effectiveness in the management of the alcoholic. Psychopharmaceutical medication, now available to control the problem drinker's anxiety and tension, often reduces the need for alcohol's tension-reducing properties and helps make the patient more accessible to psychological counseling. Drugs such as disulfiram—which sensitizes the individual to alcohol so that ingestion of even a small amount results in illness—are helpful with certain types of patients. All in all, "while alcoholism is still a very difficult disease to treat and requires much patience and detailed planning on the part of the physician, there is now a greater possibility of obtaining gratifying results than existed 10 or 15 years ago."[7]

REFERENCES CHAPTER 9

1. McCarthy, R. G., and Douglas, E. M.: *in* McCarthy, R. G., ed.: Drinking and Intoxication, Glencoe, Free Press, 1959.
2. Roueche, B.: Neutral Spirit, A Portrait of Alcohol, Boston, Little, 1960.
3. Greenblatt, Robert B.: Search the Scriptures, Philadelphia, Lippincott, 1963, Chapter 5, "A Little Wine."
4. Straus, R., and Bacon, S. D.: Drinking in College, New Haven, Yale Univ Press, 1953.
5. Coates, A.: Popular Government 4:1, 1937.
6. Chafetz, M. E., and Demone, H. W., Jr.: Alcoholism and Society, New York, Oxford, 1962.
7. Brightman, I. J.: *in* Hilleboe, H. E., and Larimore, G. W., eds.: Preventive Medicine, Philadelphia, Saunders, 1959.
8. Seliger, R. V., Cranford, V., and Goodwin, H. S.: J Clin Exp Psychopath 6:145, 1944.

CHAPTER 10

RESEARCHERS SPECULATE

WHAT MAKES an alcoholic? has been examined, within the past several years, from many viewpoints—psychological, sociologic, physiologic—with growing appreciation that this is a question with many facets. Its complexity becomes even more apparent with some of the biochemical findings relating to alcoholism. Yet, in a way, these minute and intricately interwoven observations hold most hope. From these basic studies may come some of the missing links that, considered together with all other factors, will eventually lead to more fundamental medical treatment of the disease known as alcoholism and, possibly, to clues for its prevention.

What determines, for example, whether a laboratory rat will become an "alcoholic" or a "teetotaler?" With psychological and sociologic considerations that strongly influence man pretty well ruled out, many investigators have focused on the part that dietary factors play. They find that rats can be made to turn to alcohol by manipulating food rations, vitamin supplies and calories. But in the last few years, D. A. Rodgers and G. E. McClearn, at the University of California at Berkeley, have succeeded in breeding various strains, some that prefer alcohol, some that accept it under certain conditions, others that refuse it even when their food supply is cut by 50% and when they are severely dehydrated. Why are these rats teetotalers? These experiments raise the possibility of genetic differences in susceptibility to alcoholism, but as yet the factors have not been identified.

ADDICTED CELLS

Even isolated cells grown in tissue culture can become "addicts," according to recent studies. Last year, G. Corrsen and I. A. Skora, at the University of Michigan Medical Center, published a report on experiments showing that when epithelial cells are grown in cultures to which morphine is gradually added and then withdrawn from the fluid, there are marked "withdrawal" symptoms. Some of the cells shrivel up, some die immediately; none of them can multiply, and therefore the culture dies out. This is evidence that withdrawal symptoms may be due to actual chemical changes. So far, these investigators have used morphine, but if future research shows similar results when alcohol is used, it may contribute to our understanding of alcoholism and the withdrawal syndrome in man.

METABOLIC STUDIES IN MAN

Biochemists have long looked for metabolic clues to the intoxicating effects of alcohol and to the problem of alcoholism. The enzyme alcohol dehydrogenase, in particular, has been the subject of study by a number of groups during the past ten years. Of the several thousands

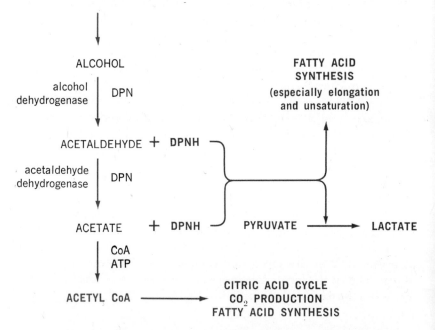

Fig. 3. Pathways in the metabolism and utilization of alcohol by the liver (*Adapted from* Isselbacher, K. J., and Greenberger, N. J.[1])

of enzymes the body produces, only three have been isolated in pure form, one of which is alcohol dehydrogenase. Since this occurs primarily in the liver, where the enzyme catalyzes the first step in the metabolism of alcohol—its oxidation to acetaldehyde—there have been both experimental and clinical investigations of alcohol dehydrogenase activity in such conditions as cirrhosis, fatty infiltration and viral hepatitis (to name just a few directions of research), but with varying conclusions. A major step forward came a couple of years ago when Bethune, Mendelson, Von Wartburg and Vallee, then working together at the Biophysics Research Laboratory, Peter Bent Brigham Hospital in Boston, succeeded in isolating alcohol dehydrogenase from human liver. Another finding is that barbiturates interfere with alcohol dehydrogenase activity—an observation that may bear on the increased fatality among patients who take heavy doses of both barbiturates and alcohol.

NEW APPROACHES TO LIVER DISEASE

The role of nutritional deficiencies in the pathogenesis of liver disease such as cirrhosis is well, if not precisely, established. Recent research also indicates a direct toxic effect of alcohol on the liver. Of alcoholic patients at the Boston City Hospital, 45% were found to have a folic acid deficiency, known to lead to megaloblastic anemia. Experimental work has shown that alcohol inhibits the development of the red blood cells because it blocks the growth-promoting action of folic acid. Alcohol also causes a partial suppression of the response of the

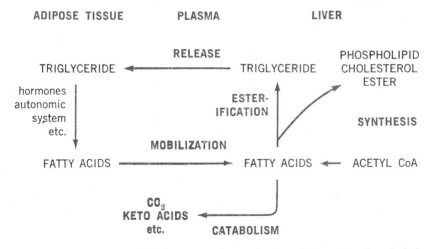

Fig. 4. Five possible factors in the production of fatty liver by alcohol (*Adapted from* Isselbacher, K. J., and Greenberger, N. J.[1])

body to vitamin B_{12} in patients with pernicious anemia. Leevy has found that alcoholics are low in both these factors and pyridoxine as well, a deficiency that may interfere with DNA synthesis and prevent regeneration of hepatic cells.

Some chronic alcoholic patients have decreased bone marrow granulocytes, even though they may not have liver disease, and severe leukopenia may occur in alcoholics after a serious bacterial infection. A direct toxic effect on the liver is also believed to occur, as evidenced by the increased transaminase found in the blood of patients with delirium tremens.

Experimental work of promise for prevention of liver disease is being done by Di Luzio at the University of Tennessee. When mice are given a very large dose of alcohol, the amount of fat in the liver cells increases rapidly and enormously—about 300% in 16 to 18 hours. Dr. Di Luzio has found several antioxidants that will prevent this accumulation of cellular fat, and if they should have the same effect in man, his findings would be extremely important.

SOME DIAGNOSES THAT MAY BE MISSED

Everyone, including the physician, is more likely to suspect alcoholism in a shabby "skid row" sort of person than in the well-dressed, job-holding family man who may come to the doctor's office or be hospitalized for treatment of some other definite disorder. But W. S. Pearson, in a survey of 100 random patients hospitalized for various disorders—not alcoholism—at North Carolina Memorial Hospital, found that 29 were probably alcoholics and 9 others suspect, judging by their answers to a questionnaire on drinking habits (sneaking or gulping drinks, morning drinking, loss of control, job or family problems). Another point made by Harold Sobel and Jerome Waye of the Mt. Sinai Hospital, New York, is that pancreatitis occurs three times as frequently in patients with cirrhosis of the liver as in noncirrhotic patients. Yet it is a diagnosis often missed.

A danger not widely enough recognized is that in many heavy drinkers a precipitous fall in blood sugar may occur after 12 to 24 hours of fasting—even lower than 10 mg% according to Norbert Freinkel of Boston City Hospital. Deep coma and even death may occur, but if the cause is recognized, treatment with intravenous glucose gets the patient immediately out of coma.

This review of some current research related to alcoholism is the substance of an interview with Ruth Fox, MD, the New York psychiatrist long known for her work with alcoholics. It can merely touch on a few of the many areas of research that may eventually lead to better understanding of alcoholism and its effects. The biochemical, neuro-chemical and other experimental literature pertaining to this subject is vast, and the few investigators mentioned in the text have many col-leagues who have contributed similarly to basic research. The two references for this Chapter are to recent reviews.

REFERENCES CHAPTER 10

1. Isselbacher, K. J., and Greenberger, N. J.: Metabolic effects of alcohol on the liver, New Eng J Med 270:351, 402, 1964.
2. Mendelson, J. H., ed.: Experimentally induced chronic intoxication and withdrawal in alcoholics, Quart J Stud Alcohol (Suppl 2), May, 1964.

CHAPTER 11

DRUG TREATMENT IN GENERAL PRACTICE

D RUG TREATMENT of alcoholism must meet two distinct phases: acute intoxication and its sequelae, and the basic disease entity. The first therapy is immediate and primarily physiologic and symptomatic. The second is long-range and etiologic. What is the causative mechanism of alcoholic addiction? Here, of course, is the main obstacle: this illness, causing untold suffering to millions of people, has no clear etiology, physiologic or psychological, to provide effective leverage for corrective therapy.

SOMATIC? PSYCHOLOGICAL?

Although Kissen,[1] in his discussion of the causes of alcoholism, points to "some evidence of differences in the metabolism of alcohol in the alcoholic and the nonalcoholic," Gelber,[2] summarizes the more important concepts of a somatic etiology:

A physiologically oriented school attributes alcoholism to a bio-chemical defect which produces an uncontrollable desire for alcohol—there are a number of proponents of this theory who have considered it due to a genetotrophic lack of nutritive elements, defective endocrine functions, marked food sensitivity and others.

Thus, while the possibility of a physiologic basis for alcohol addiction may exist, there is "insufficient evidence at this time to restrict treatment to an attempt to correct the bio-chemical defect." [2]

That the alcoholic has many and varied psychological problems is, on the other hand, universally accepted.[1] A psychologically oriented school sees alcoholism as a manifestation of a neurosis based on a defective or arrested development of personality in the early formative years: "certan environmental factors favor inebriety as a defense against unconscious drives connected with the personal and social life. . . ." [2] Workers may disagree on how many of these problems are caused by basic personality and neurotic patterns and how many by biochemistry,[1] but the gravity and urgency of the drinker's basic emotional difficulties cannot be denied.

"DRYING-OUT" PERIOD

The immediate objectives in the treatment of acute alcoholism, as stated by Kissen, are *1.* to get the patient sober as quickly and painlessly as possible, and *2.* to discover any intercurrent medical or psychiatric complications.[3]

In accomplishing the first objective, some of the newer tranquilizers have been remarkably effective.[1, 3-9] They expedite the resolution of the acute toxic state, rendering the patient ambulatory and capable of self-care, often within 24 hours.[6] The rapid response of disabling symptoms to chlordiazepoxide hydrochloride, for instance, is shown in Figure 5.

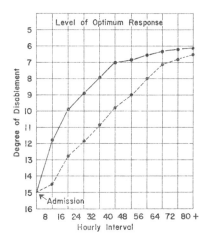

Fig. 5. Rate at which resolution of disablement occurred after administration of chlordiazepoxide HCl, evaluated at 8-hour intervals. Solid line records the results in 39 acutely intoxicated patients in the chlordiazepoxide group. Their measurements are based on recordings of nervousness, tremor, appearance, sleep, depression and appetite; after 40 hours 53.8%, and after 80 hours 90%, had reached "optimum response level." [3] Broken line records the results in 37 control patients receiving placebo, barbituates, phenothiazines and other tranquilizers. (*Adapted from* Kissen, M.D.[3])

The results are based on a hospital study of 39 acutely intoxicated patients who received 100 mg of chlordiazepoxide hydrochloride intravenously, intramuscularly or orally (at bedtime if admitted during the day; Stat. if admitted at night), followed by 10 mg of the drug by mouth four times daily for the remainder of the hospital stay.[3]

At the same time, the care or prevention of medical complications calls for fluid replacement, correction of salt deficiencies and nutritional supplementation. Thus in the patient group receiving chlordiazepoxide HCl, each patient was also given routinely: *upon admission,*

1,000 cc of 10% glucose in water and 1,000 cc of 5% glucose in saline (both solutions containing vitamin B complex); *12 hours later,* intravenously, an additional 1,000 of 10% glucose; *daily* throughout the period of hospitalization, 100 mg thiamine HCl intramuscularly, as well as other vitamin B fractions and ascorbic acid, orally.[3]

In selected cases, chloral hydrate (1 to 2 Gm) may be administered at bedtime to provide, in combination with the tranquilizer, more restful sleep.[7] The need for corticosteroids is greatly decreased in patients on tranquilizing therapy.[10] To avoid aggravating the usual gastritis, diet may be liquid for 24 hours, then soft.[11] (Specific data on dosage and on patients assigned to the therapeutic methods are not enumerated in the original report).

IS HOSPITALIZATION ADVISABLE?

Although many physicians are reluctant to treat alcoholism, perhaps feeling doubtful of their competence in handling this special problem, Kissen states: "I can assure you that any alert, well-trained general practitioner can treat alcoholism." [3] For the care of the acutely intoxicated, he feels hospitalization to be the more practical method—if only to keep the patient during the withdrawal period in a place "where the next drink that has become so important as to exclude everything else in his life cannot be gotten." [3]

Much depends also on the severity of the intoxication, on possible complications, and the general circumstances in the patient's home. In alcoholic coma or severe hallucinations and delirium tremens, while quick and vigorous emergency measures may be administered by the first attending physician, subsequent hospitalization will usually be necessary. In milder intoxications, as long as the two primary requirements—sleep and rapid restoration of a normal nutritional pattern—can be complied with in the home, hospitalization may be avoided. Here again, the remarkable effectiveness of certain tranquilizers in dramatically shortening the "soberization" period and making even severely intoxicated patients routinely manageable, may tip the balance. Pushing of fluids by mouth, for instance, frequently becomes feasible quickly under tranquilizing therapy.[7]

THE LONG ROAD TO REHABILITATION

Once the acute phase is under control and the patient begins to feel "human" again, efforts are made to plan, and discuss with him, the long-range program of rehabilitation. This treatment must include medical and psychological approaches. Psychologically, the long-term treatment of alcoholism is described as directed toward the achievement of these ends [1]: *1. identification by the patient* himself as an alcoholic, *2. surrender by the patient* to the fact that any quantity of alcohol taken will lead to his particular pattern of binge drinking, and *3. realization by the patient* of the egocentricity of alcoholic behavior and of the need for creating meaningful social relationships.

It is essential also that the patient be aware of the pattern of complete sobriety that he must follow. He should be prepared, mentally and physically, for the increased anxiety reactions and tensions that he is going to face.[1, 12] This is particularly important, because the alcoholic is by nature vulnerable to psychic distress and has low tolerance for psychic pain.[10] Observations on alcoholics stress the pattern of constant anxiety and tension that gradually build up to a level of intolerable discomfort—the point at which the patient resorts to alcohol for relief. This anxiety is usually quite obvious to both the medical observer and the patient himself. Even in individuals who denied feeling nervous and tense, the Minnesota Multiphasic Personality Inventory showed characteristic indications of a high anxiety level.[13]

BLUNTING ANXIETIES AND TENSIONS

Two medical therapies have greatly increased the physician's success in fortifying the alcoholic's resistance to drinking: the tranquilizers and disulfiram. Tranquilizing drugs, Block finds,[14] help the patient to overcome tensions that he formerly relieved by using alcohol. Carefully selected and controlled, they may take the edge off the anxiety or depression that threatens to make the patient desert sobriety.[15] While a danger of starting a substitution habit may exist with some of the tranquilizers, Mead feels that with reasonable caution this risk can be eliminated.[15] Barbiturates, on the other hand, should be avoided because of the ease with which the alcoholic can become first habituated, and then addicted, to them.[16]

Another decided advantage of tranquilizing therapy is its observed ability to make alcoholic patients more productive in psychotherapeutic interviews and to lend what appears to be a greater capacity for objective appraisal of their problems and life situations.[8]

The other development of possible usefulness in the long-range control of alcoholism, disulfiram, establishes a fear of alcohol by linking the consumption of alcoholic beverages with nausea, vomiting and the severe discomforts of vasomotor phenomena. Its effectiveness as an alcohol-sensitizing drug was discovered quite accidentally when, in their search for an anthelmintic, two Danish researchers, Drs. Jacobsen and Hald, dosed themselves with tetraethylthiuram disulfide. Soon after, while having a cocktail at a party, they startled the company by developing tachycardia, dyspnea, a lobster-like complexion and red bulging eyes—now recognized as the alcohol-disulfiram reaction.[10]

Increasing familiarity with disulfiram and adjustment of dosage has markedly reduced the incidence of disabling side-effects that had attended its indiscriminate use in the earlier phases.[10] Still, close medical supervision of the patient is indicated. The main contraindications are severe cardiovascular illness, hepatic cirrhosis, epilepsy, drug addiction, psychoses, kidney disease, diabetes, pregnancy and asthma.[4] Caution is also indicated in applying general anesthesia to the disulfiram patient.[17] Among antidotes, antihistamines, ascorbic acid and measures against vasomotor collapse are recommended.[4, 18, 19]

When this treatment was first used, disulfiram was administered for about a week, and then the patient was given some alcoholic beverage so that he might experience the effect alcohol would have on him in the future. For some time now, it has been thought unnecessary to subject patients to such an experience. There are two reasons for this: the possibility of misleading, and falsely reassuring, the patient by a *mild* reaction; the difficulty of anticipating the severity of a *strong* reaction, even if planned.[8] The mere description of what will happen, and the fact that he is given a card to carry with him explaining that,

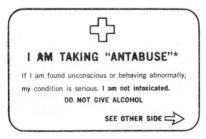

Fig. 6. Card given to Antabuse patients (*From* Stroup, *et al.:* Appl Ther 7:550, 1965)

if found unconscious, no alcohol should be given him, usually suffice to impress the patient with the seriousness of this treatment.[4]

IS A "PHARMACOLOGIC FENCE" PRACTICAL?

The question has been raised whether disulfiram can actually build a "pharmacologic fence" around the patient, thereby relieving him of the responsibility for abstinence. In the opinion of E. C. Hoff, this is not feasible: "the alcoholic can never permanently delegate to any other person or modality the privilege and responsibility of his own decision about abstaining."[9] Actually, even when on long-range disulfiram therapy, the patient must renew daily his acceptance of the fact that he cannot drink and, in token thereof, take the medication.

However, disulfiram may be looked on as a deterrent to the occasional impulsive relapse because the patient's mood may change by the time he knows that it is safe to drink again.[20] "I still get in rages against my husband and against my psychiatrist," comments a disulfiram patient, "and, always before, when I was angry like that, I would get drunk. Now I can't, and by the time I can, if I stop the pills, I'm not angry any more and so I start the pills again."[18] Still, even with this "somatic" safeguard, the predominance of psychological factors remains apparent. In controlled experiments, the patients preferring disulfiram consistently constituted the younger, healthier and, possibly, more highly motivated groups. They were the patients who were generally more cooperative and more desirous of being helped to stop drinking in the first place.[9, 21] The drug was rejected by older patients and those with more profound deterioration.[9]

The conditioned reflex treatment of Voegtlin is still another method of associating physical distress with alcohol intake. The treatment consists in giving the patient alcohol to which an emetic has been added. This is repeated in a well-set routine until the patient becomes nauseous simply on seeing or smelling alcoholic beverages. The strictly controlled circumstances needed to establish this conditioned response limit the treatment to institutions.[4, 10, 20] Finally, vitamins, hormones, high-protein and high-caloric diets have their places in a comprehensive management. It is estimated that 25% of the patients starting treatment for chronic alcoholism show evidence of moderate to severe malnutrition—physical symptoms associated with nutritional depletion, felt by many to be related to liver damage—as well as paresthesias of the extremities due to peripheral neuritis.[20]

AVOIDING THAT "ONE DRINK"

A sincere wish to be cured is essential to the successful treatment of alcoholism. This can often be aroused by the empathy and patience of an understanding physician—who must, at the same time, demand strict adherence to his prescribed regimen. The patient must understand that the doctor will not condone his drinking: it is the "one drink" that can make the difference between the successfully treated case and the unsuccessful one.

Can this temptation be withstood indefinitely? With the therapies at hand, there is no longer reason for a hopeless attitude about alcoholism. The tranquilizing drugs have greatly simplified the treatment of acute alcoholism; and through their long-range use, the patient can be kept more comfortable emotionally, have a chance to gain insight into his problems, and possibly learn to cope with them. At critical moments, recourse may be had to disulfiram in enforcing motivation. Finally, maintaining the alcoholic at optimum physical fitness will in itself make him feel better and more capable of staying on his long road to rigid sobriety.

REFERENCES CHAPTER 11

1. Kissen, M. D.: Quart J Stud Alcohol Suppl *1*:101, 1961.
2. Gelber, I.: Alcoholism in New York City, The City of New York, Dept of Health, 1960, pp. 24 ff.
3. Kissen, M. D.: Missouri Med *59*:965, 1962.
4. Block, M. A.: *in* Manual on Alcoholism by the Committee on Alcoholism, Chicago, Amer Med Ass, 1957, pp. 8 ff.
5. Major, R. A.: GP *21*:104 (2), 1960.
6. Chambers, J. F., and Schultz, J. D.: Quart J Stud Alcohol *26*:10, 1965.
7. Schultz, J. D.: Quart J Stud Alcohol Suppl *1*:85, 1961.
8. Lawrence, F. E.: Quart J Stud Alcohol Suppl *1*:117, 1961.
9. Hoff, E. C.: Quart J Stud Alcohol Suppl *1*:138, 1961.
10. Pfeffer, A. Z.: Alcoholism, New York, Grune, 1958, pp. 12, 29 ff., 52 ff.
11. Bell, E. F.: J Mississippi Med Ass *4*:200, 1963.
12. Smith, J. A.: Quart J Stud Alcohol Suppl *1*:129, 1961.
13. Haden, H.: Psychosomatics *2*:279, 1961.
14. Block, M. A.: New York J Med *61*:2561, 1961.
15. Mead, B. T.: S Dakota J Med Pharm *14*:420, 1961.
16. Block, M. A.: Med Times *90*:381, 1962.
17. Allen, E. B., and Prout, C. T.: Progr Neurol Psychiat *8*:486, 1953.
18. Feldman, D. J., and Zucker, H. D.: JAMA *153*:895, 1953.
19. Kant, F.: The Treatment of the Alcoholic, Springfield (Ill.), Thomas, 1954, pp. 87 ff.
20. Ewalt, J. R., Strecker, E. A., and Ebaugh, F. G.: Practical Clinical Psychiatry, ed. 8, New York, McGraw-Hill, 1957, pp. 364 ff.
21. Wallace, J. A.: Quart J Stud Alcohol *13*:397, 1952.

CHAPTER 12

THE ROLE OF THE FAMILY DOCTOR

IN THE COURSE of a week, some family doctors often see five to ten patients who are either already alcoholics or well on their way. Usually, the doctor himself spots the warning signs: the patient has one of the suspicion-arousing illnesses, such as gastritis, perhaps, and seems to have trouble holding a job. In some cases, a 'phone call precedes the patient's visit and a harried wife or exasperated employer urges the doctor to "please talk to John about his drinking!"

With diplomacy, judgment and careful history-taking, the doctor soon establishes that his patient does indeed have a serious drinking problem. However—what then? Alcoholics are notoriously uncooperative individuals, and physicians are notoriously short of time. The temptation is strong simply to treat any existing physical disorders, inform the patient of the severe medical complications that he can expect if he continues to drink heavily, and then send him on his way.

But it is often a mistake to give in to this temptation. As Bates [1] points out, alcoholics have a potentially fatal disease. Moreover, their condition is not so untreatable as it is commonly believed. "Terminal cancer and leukemia are hopeless," Bates wryly observes, "but alcoholism can be arrested in at least 50% of the cases who come for help." Thimann [2] agrees that alcoholics can and do respond well to a medical regimen under the supervision of an interested family physician. While he estimates that 30% of the alcoholic population may be psychotic or severely psychoneurotic, and may require psychiatric care, the remaining 70% are only mildly psychoneurotic: "an amazing number of such alcoholics have remained sober and have matured psychologically without the aid of orthodox psychotherapy."

THE "DIFFICULT" PATIENT

Success is not easily achieved, of course, with the alcoholic. As a rule, he tends to be an impulsive, immature and easily discouraged individual. Then, too, the choice he is being asked to make—between a life of complete sobriety and a life of uncontrolled drinking—is not as simple as it seems. To the alcoholic, it often appears to be a choice between "(a) unbearable tension, self-disgust, inadequacy in every activity, deep depression, and even suicide; or (b) calm, euphoria, blurred reality, and high self-esteem to the point of omnipotence, or self-approval for gratification of impulses otherwise inhibited." [3]

Such a patient can be expected, obviously, to "protect" his alcoholism as zealously as he can, to rationalize his frequent relapses, even to deny that he has a drinking problem despite evidence that, to others, is incontrovertible. Nevertheless, he does know that something is wrong in his life and, like most unhappy people, is desperately anxious to find someone who will understand his miseries and discomforts.

"Perhaps the greatest contribution that the personal physician can make," Block suggests,[4] "is early detection of the illness in his patient and the ability to listen to him while the patient ventilates the many problems which face him."

Deep probing of the alcoholic's underlying conflicts is usually unnecessary.[5] Discussion of his day-to-day problems—with his wife, his job, his financial situation—can be done on a practical, common-sense level, with the fact that alcohol plays an important role in creating his problems repeatedly emphasized. In essence, the brief counseling sessions might be considered a reeducation program: designed to help the alcoholic see himself and his problems more realistically and to learn to cope with his difficulties in more mature and constructive ways. Medication available to assist the doctor in his attempts to rehabilitate the chronic alcoholic falls into two broad categories: tranquilizers and deterrent agents, discussed in Chapter 11.

THE "FAMILY ILLNESS"

In the case of acute alcoholism, the most shattering aftereffects are often seen in the patient's family, and its members may be in need of the physician's guidance and support more urgently than the patient himself. While the alcoholic may not be ready to admit that he needs help, his wife or children may be on the verge of emotional collapse.

The doctor's counsel can do much to restore the family's psychological balance and to encourage the development of a more realistic attitude toward alcoholism. He should stress that the alcoholic member of the family is truly a sick person, that treatment programs *can* help him, and that he must be encouraged to avail himself of them. And the family should be informed of the organizations, such as Alcoholics Anonymous, established to help persons in their situation.

In addition, the alert physician may discover that certain family members are unconsciously acting in ways that promote the patient's continued drinking.[6] He may suspect, for instance, that a wife appears to be enjoying her role as martyr or might actually prefer her husband sodden but dependent. Such circumstances naturally require extremely tactful handling but, when well managed, can improve the alcoholic's chances for rehabilitation.

WHEN REFERRAL IS NECESSARY

Although the family doctor is responsible for the overall management of the alcoholic patient, he has a number of "therapeutic assistants" in the specialties and in various social and civic agencies. In some cases—despite the severe shortage of psychiatrists in many communities—he may decide that a psychiatric referral is essential, particularly when there is a question of psychosis. More often, he may simply want psychiatric advice on the handling of the alcoholic or the support of his family where there is more than usual complexity.

Close to 200 communities now have outpatient clinics and counseling services, many of them supported by state or county. The patient referred to one of these clinics may be given supportive counseling or brief psychotherapy. Social workers attached to the clinics can render valuable assistance to the alcoholic's family. (Both the American Medical Association and the National Council on Alcoholism publish directories listing resources for help in management of alcoholism in the various states.) A number of private clinics also specialize in the rehabilitation of alcoholics and might be the answer when cost is not a consideration.

Alcoholics Anonymous, with more than 7,000 local chapters, is undoubtedly the best known and most widely available resource. For a number of alcoholics, AA provides a social milieu in which they can feel accepted and can talk to others with problems very like their own.

Certain individuals, however, can accept neither the organization's spiritual approach nor its intense group life. In any case, if the patient goes to AA, Moore advises, "medical responsibility is not reduced and contacts should be maintained." [6]

THE PRIME RESPONSIBILITY

That the family doctor has a prime responsibility in the treatment of alcoholism is rarely disputed today. In a recent poll of 161 midwestern physicians,[7] all but a few believed that they had the same responsibility in the treatment of alcoholism as they had in any other illness. As physicians, they must, of course, treat the acute phase and the resulting physical disabilities. Many also felt that their responsibility included help in interpersonal relationships, psychotherapy, counseling of the patient and his family, and referral of the patient to other appropriate sources. These physicians, and others throughout the country, clearly have come to recognize the truth of Yvelin Gardner's statement: "More often than not, the family doctor holds the fate of the alcoholic in his hands." [8]

REFERENCES CHAPTER 12

1. Bates, R. C.: J Mich Med Soc 62:1009, 1963.
2. Thimann, J.: Quart J Stud Alcohol 26:310, 1965.
3. Moore, R. A.: Med Times 91:1143, 1963.
4. Block, M. A.: New York J Med 61:2561, 1961.
5. Selzer, M. L.: J Mich Med Soc 62:981, 1963.
6. Moore, R. A.: J Mich Med Soc 62:50, 1963.
7. Johnson, M. W.: Nebraska Med J 50:378, 1965.
8. Gardner, Y.: Med Times 89:27, 1961.

INDEX

79